The **Mini Rough Guide** to

ISTANBUL & THE AEGEAN COAST

ROUGH GUIDES

How to download your Free eBook

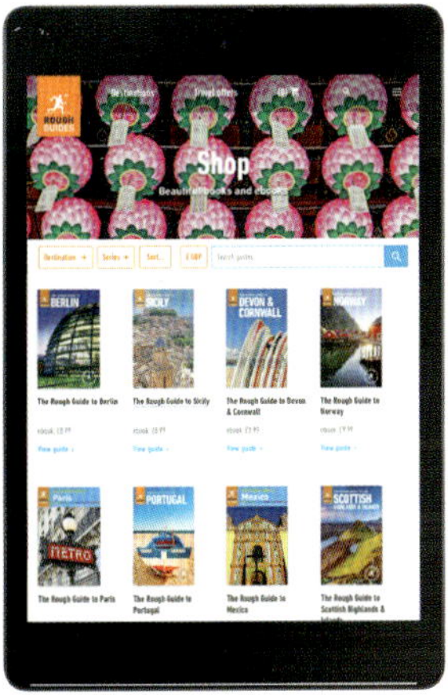

1. Visit **www.roughguides.com/free-ebook** or scan the **QR code** opposite

2. Enter the code **istanbul730**

3. Follow the simple step-by-step instructions

For troubleshooting contact: mail@roughguides.com

Contents

Introduction

Istanbul is one of the world's most atmospheric cities. Part of the allure is its setting, where Europe faces Asia across the waters of the Bosphorus, making it the only city in the world to bridge two continents. Here, where the Black Sea blends into the Aegean, East and West mingle and merge in the cultural melting pot of Turkey's largest metropolis. Oriental bazaars co-exist with European shops and malls; kebab shops and teahouses sit alongside stylish brasseries; sleek glass-fronted office buildings and hotels alternate with Ottoman minarets along the city's skyline; traditional music and Western pop, belly-dancing and ballet, Turkish wrestling and football all compete for the attention of the *İstanbullu* audience.

Stopping for a drink in a Beyoğlu backstreet

This is the only city in the world to have been the capital of both an Islamic and a Christian empire. As Constantinople, jewel of the Byzantine Empire, it was for more than 1,000 years the most important city in Christendom. As Istanbul it was the seat of the Ottoman sultans, rulers of a 500-year Islamic empire that stretched from the Black Sea and the Balkans to Arabia and Algeria.

This cross-fertilisation of ideas, neither European nor Oriental, has created one of the world's most engaging and hospitable cultures.

WHAT'S NEW

Some of the most notable recent developments in Istanbul are actually new chapters in very old stories. In 2020, Hagia Sophia (see page 36) became a mosque again for the first time since 1935, having been a museum and then a church. Also in 2020, the Byzantine Kariye Church, most recently a museum, also became a mosque (see page 59). In 2024, the Bulgur Palas, a long-closed mansion, re-opened as a cultural centre and library, as part of a plan to restore several historic buildings in Istanbul. Another restoration is the Gülhane Park Cistern, an ancient underground vaulted water management system from the 5th century, which opened To the public in 2023. The same year saw Casa Botter, the Art Nouveau former home of Dutch fashion designer Jean Botter, open as a gallery and design centre.

STRATEGIC LOCATION

Istanbul's historical significance is due to its strategic location at the mouth of the Bosphorus. From this vantage point, the city could control the ships that passed through the strait on the trade route between the Black Sea and the Mediterranean, and the overland traffic from Europe to Asia Minor that used the strait as a crossing point. In the words of the 16th-century French traveller Pierre Gilles: 'The Bosphorus with one key opens and closes two worlds, two seas.'

That strategic advantage is no less important today than it was 2,500 years ago, when a band of Greeks first founded the city of Byzantium on this spot. Ankara is the official capital of modern Turkey, but Istanbul remains the country's largest city, most important commercial and industrial centre, and busiest port, accounting for more than one-third of Turkey's manufacturing output. The Bosphorus is one of the world's most active shipping lanes, and the overland traffic is carried by two of the world's longest suspension bridges.

URBAN CONTRASTS

The city has long since spread beyond the 5th-century Byzantine walls built by Emperor Theodosius II and now sprawls for miles along the shores of the Sea of Marmara on both the European and Asian sides. In 1507 this was the world's largest city, with a population of 1.2 million. That figure has now passed 15 million and is still growing, swollen by a steady influx of people from rural areas (more than half the population was born in the provinces). These new arrivals have created a series of shanty towns around the perimeter of the city. Their makeshift homes, known as *gecekondu* ('built by night'), take advantage of an old Ottoman law that protects a house whose roof has been built during the hours of darkness. The slums are eventually knocked down to make way for new tower blocks – a new suburb is created, yet another shanty town springs up beyond it, and Istanbul spreads out a little farther. In addition, run-down neighbourhoods are being spruced up by the

WHEN TO GO

Istanbul's climate exhibits strong seasonality, varying a lot over the course of the year – and, as befits its position at the crossroads of two continents, the weather generally is a bridge between the mild coastal Mediterranean and harsher temperatures of Anatolia. The weather will likely influence what time of year you wish to visit. Winters have the benefit of smaller crowds, but are often chilly, and the coastal location means there can be a lot of rain and even snow. High summer, meanwhile, can be uncomfortably hot and humid, not to mention extremely busy, being the peak tourist season. That said, summer is a good time for festivals, like the Istanbul Music Festival and Victory Day celebrations. On balance, many visitors find that the best times to visit Istanbul are the shoulder seasons of spring (when the Tulip Festival adds a splash of colour to the city's public spaces) and autumn.

council, with subsequent leaps in property values that force out poorer residents.

At the other end of the social spectrum are the wealthy *İstanbullus*, who live in the up-market districts of Taksim, Harbiye and Nişantaşı, where the streets are lined with fashion boutiques, expensive apartments and stylish cafés. Members of this set are the lucky few who frequent the city's more expensive restaurants and casinos, and retire at the weekends to their *yalı* (restored wooden mansions) along the Bosphorus. But most of Istanbul's inhabitants fall between these two extremes, living in modest flats and earning an average wage – lower than in the rest of the Europe – in the offices, shops, banks and factories that provide most of the city's employment.

Although small Armenian, Greek Orthodox, Jewish and Catholic communities survive, the majority of *İstanbullus* are Muslim and adhere to the

Traditional Islamic clothing in Istanbul

NOTES

The word 'Turkey' relates to both a country and a festive dinner: is there a relationship? The succulent birds originated in the Americas; meanwhile, Turks call a turkey a 'hindi'. However, the 17th-century ruler of the Mughal Empire of Pakistan and India did possess a painting of a turkey – it's possible he imported them and then exported to Turkey.

principles known as the 'Five Pillars of Islam' – to believe with all one's heart that 'There is no God but Allah, and Mohammed is his Prophet'; to pray five times a day, at dawn, midday, afternoon, sunset and after dark; to give alms to the poor and towards the upkeep of the mosques; to fast between sunrise and sunset during the month of Ramadan; and to try to make the pilgrimage to Mecca at least once.

Islam in Turkey is, on the whole, an open, welcoming brand of the religion, where the visitor is made to feel at home (able to go into mosques, for example). The secular society created by Atatürk is clearly visible in the contemporary culture and fashion followed by both men and women. However, there is creeping conservatism among the poor, more traditional population, and the ruling

Inside the Byzantine Hagia Sophia

SUSTAINABLE TRAVEL

Walking is a great way to get around Istanbul, with the crammed-in nature of the Old City meaning many attractions are reachable on foot. The metro is another efficient and eco-friendly way to get around. Out towards the Aegean coast, cycling becomes a more viable option, and is a lovely way to explore archaeological sites like Ephesus, coastal resorts such as Bodrum (see page 96), and nature reserves like Dilek National Park (see page 91). Hotels and resorts will often have bicycles available to rent. On the other hand, the availability of plant-based meals diminishes significantly once you get out of Istanbul.

AKP party that has been gradually drifting apart from the secular state, turning iconic buildings like Hagia Sophia and Chora back into mosques.

PRINCIPAL ATTRACTIONS

Just as the Bosphorus separates Asia from Europe, so the inlet called the *haliç* (Golden Horn) separates old Istanbul from the new. The main attractions for the visitor are concentrated in old Istanbul. Three great civilisations have shaped this part of the city – Roman, Byzantine and Ottoman. Though little remains from Roman times, the city's Byzantine legacy includes Hagia Sophia, one of the world's greatest buildings; the magnificent mosaics of St Saviour in Chora; and the impressive Theodosian Walls. The Ottomans built countless mosques, the finest being Süleymaniye Camii, built by Turkey's greatest architect, Sinan. But the most popular tourist sight is Topkapı Palace, home of the Ottoman sultans. From the belvedere in the palace treasury, you can look across the mouth of the Golden Horn to the modern district of Beyoğlu, surrounding the turret of the Galata Tower. Round the corner, by the Bosphorus, is the 19th-century Dolmabahçe Palace, while beyond stretches the span of the Bosphorus Bridge.

10 Things not to miss

1 **BOSPHORUS BY FERRY**
A trip along the famous strait, with lots to see on the way. See page 74.

2 **SÜLEYMANIYE MOSQUE**
The finest Ottoman building in Istanbul. See page 55.

3 **KARIYE MOSQUE**
One of Istanbul's greatest Byzantine buildings. See page 59.

4 **GRAND BAZAAR**
The largest covered market in the world, with 4,000 shops. See page 53.

5 **EPHESUS**
One of the best-preserved ancient sites in Turkey and the top historical attraction along the Aegean coast. See page 91.

6 **BASILICA CISTERN**
Part of the city's Byzantine-era system of underground reservoirs. See page 51.

7 **JANISSARY BAND CONCERT**
Reviving days of Ottoman glory in spectacular fashion. See page 69.

8 **TOPKAPI PALACE**
Richly adorned home of the sultans and their harem. See page 42.

9 **HAGIA SOPHIA**
Completed in AD537 and still one of the world's greatest architectural wonders. See page 36.

10 **İSTIKLAL CADDESI**
At the heart of the lively, European-style New City. See page 67.

A perfect day in Istanbul

8.00AM

Breakfast. Enjoy a Turkish breakfast in your hotel or a local café – lots of fresh bread, white cheese, honey, and gallons of black tea.

9.00AM

Hagia Sophia. Walk up the steps to the gallery of this architectural wonder (see page 36) for a closer look at the 13th-century mosaic of 'Christ Pantocrator', flanked by the Virgin Mary and John the Baptist.

12.00PM

Archaeology. Stroll to the Archaeological Museum (see page 47) and marvel at the Babylonian-era frescoes, the mammoth marble statues and Mehmet II's tiled Pavilion.

1.30PM

Süleymaniye Mosque. Walk up Divan Yolu, following the tramline to this immense mosque (see page 52). After you've gazed inside Sinan's masterpiece, visit the tombs of Süleyman and his wife Roxelana, in the rose-strewn graveyard, then eat tasty *fasülye* beans for lunch.

3.00PM

Grand Bazaar. Enter the bustling 500-year-old bazaar (see page 53), the world's largest covered market, to explore narrow alleyways crammed with treasures. If you need a break from shopping, head to the Old Bedestenfor a cappuccino in a choice of smart little cafés.

5.00PM

Markets. Walk down the trading streets to busy Eminönü (see page 34), to the Egyptian (Spice) Market and Yeni Camii (New Mosque). Buy *lokum* (Turkish delight), peruse the outdoor stalls, then try a *balik ekmek* (fish sandwich), filled with fish straight from the fishing boats.

6.00PM

Panoramic views. Cross Galata Bridge, past lines of fishermen. Walk uphill to the Galata Tower (see page 66), or take the tiny funicular from Karaköy to Tünel. Ascend the sturdy tower for a fantastic view over the city.

6.30PM

Sundowner in Tünel. Walk up Galipdede Sokak, a narrow street of music shops, with traditional instruments hanging in the windows, to Tünel, a bohemian nightlife area filled with café-bars and tucked-away wine bars, perfect for an aperitif. Browse bookstores along İstiklal Caddesi or rummage for discounted designer clothes in Iş Merkezi.

8.00PM

After dark. Head to busy Nevizade Sokak for a lively *meyhane* (tavern) to feast on fresh fish, or take your pick along İstiklal Caddesi for Thai fusion or good old Turkish home cooking. Then take the elevator up to ever-so-trendy 360 Istanbul (see page 106), for rooftop cocktails and dancing.

Istanbul on a budget

8.00AM

Morning feast. Lavish breakfasts are a mainstay of many Turkish hotels, but you can find one much more cheaply at the aptly named Breakfast Street in the Beşiktaş neighbourhood, lined with eateries serving affordable platters of bread and cheese, *menemen* (scrambled eggs) and pişi (fried dough balls). Walk it off in Maçka Democracy Park.

10.00AM

Explore on foot. Walk down to the waterfront and turn right, in the direction of the Galata neighbourhood (see page 66). You'll pass a number of free attractions heading this way, including vibrant street art splashed on sets of stairs – first the so-called Rainbow Steps, and then another staircase painted with a mural of a woman in traditional dress. Arriving in the Galata neighbourhood, admire the famous Galata Tower.

12.00PM

Culture hit. Before lunch, spend a couple of hours in SALT Galata (see page 66), a cultural centre and art gallery which is completely free to enter. Housed in a grand building that was once the Ottoman Bank, SALT is now home to a library, a café, and an exhibition space.

2.00PM

Historic sites. Cross the iconic Galata Bridge, over the equally iconic Bosphorus Strait, into the Sultanahmet district, a jewel box of Ottoman, Byzantine and Roman history. You'll be hungry by now, so first port of call is lunch – luckily, Eminönü, the waterfront neighbourhood beside the bridge, has no end of food stalls.

3.00PM

Jewel of Istanbul. Close to Eminönü is the Suleymaniye Mosque (see page 56). With its spear-like towers, bubble-shaped domes and soaring arches, this is one of the most beautiful buildings in Istanbul, and it's completely free to enter – just be aware that it closes to non-Muslims during prayer time.

4.30PM

Spice market. A short walk from the mosque you'll find one of Istanbul's most captivating destinations. The Egyptian Bazaar (see page 35), also known as the Spice Bazaar, is a feast for the senses, with the aroma of rosewater perfumes mingling with exotic herbs and spices that line the shopfronts. You'll also find coffee and honey here, as well as plenty of shops selling souvenirs.

6.00PM

People-watching. The surrounding Sultanahmet neighbourhood is also where you'll find clues to Istanbul's ancient past, with the Sultanahmet Square occupying the site of the former Roman Hippodrome. The impressive Ancient Egyptian Obelisk of Theodosius still stands here, as it has since the 4th century AD, and is a great place to people-watch as the sun goes down on Istanbul.

Istanbul for foodies

8.00AM

Try gözleme. Istanbul stakes its claim as a great foodie city from virtually the moment you wake up. Nowhere does breakfast quite like Turkey – it's not uncommon to sit down and be presented with more platters of food that can even fit on the table. Try Bereket Mantı Ve Gözleme Evi, in the Eyüp neighbourhood, and be sure to try the signature gözleme – turnovers stuffed with meat, cheese, and vegetables.

10.00AM

Aromatic coffee. Turkish coffee is one of the characteristic sights and aromas of Istanbul. Strong, thick, grainy and dark, many visitors find it to be an acquired taste, but it's one you should definitely try during your time here. Head to Eyüp station and ride the cable car up Pierre Loti Hill, named for the French novelist of the same name who wrote evocatively about Istanbul. Here you'll find the Pierre Loti Café (see page 64), an atmospheric old place which serves great coffee with sweeping views over the Golden Horn.

2.00PM

Browse a bazaar. As befits its status as a trading city at the crossroads of Europe and Asia, Istanbul has some truly great markets. The most well-known is the Egyptian Bazaar (see page 35), which is a must-visit for any foodie in Istanbul. Built in the 17th century, it was originally a spice market and has now expanded to sell all manner of produce, from fruit, nuts and perfumes to the classic Turkish confectionary, *lokum*, also known as Turkish Delight. Don't miss the chance to try this sweet treat, often flavoured with pistachio and rosewater.

4.00PM

Snack time. From Eminönü, near the Egyptian Bazaar, take a boat across the Bosphorus to Kadıköy, a waterfront neighbourhood on the Asian side of Istanbul where you'll find some of the city's best street food. Another of Istanbul's great bazaars, Kadıköy Market, is a good place to start, with stalls piled high with seasonal fruits and *lüfer* (bluefish) fresh from the Bosphorus. Outside the market, you'll find many stalls selling *pide*, a classic Turkish thin flatbread topped with meat, cheese and vegetables.

6.00PM

Wine and platters. You'll have been on your feet a while now, so take a seat in the leafy garden of Viktor Levi, a café and wine bar not far from the market. Turkish wine is not well known internationally, but has an ancient history, and a number of producers are reviving old traditions, particularly in the Cappadocia region of Anatolia. One unusual thing to try is sour cherry wine, a strong, sweet fortified wine. Taking a ferry back across the Bosphorus, see out your foodie tour at Queb, an acclaimed rooftop restaurant where delicious grilled platters are served overlooking the Sultanahmet skyline.

History

Byzas, the legendary founder of Byzantium, was the son of the sea god Poseidon. In around 660BC, the oracle at Delphi told him to settle an area on the western shore of the Bosphorus. Surrounded by water on three sides, the site not only occupied a perfect strategic location, but was an ideal spot for trade. Topkapı Palace, transport hubs and bazaars occupy this spot today.

Centuries earlier, Jason and the Argonauts, seeking the Golden Fleece, had rowed through the Bosphorus following a pigeon, and escaped the clashing rocks, which threatened to kill them. The rocks never clashed again. Could this myth have grown from an earthquake, which are common here?

Ancient ruins at Priene

The shores of the Aegean are equally fabled. The Trojan War stemmed from Paris's love for Helen of Troy. The ancient Greeks took the fall of Troy, as recounted by Homer, as the starting point of their history.

AEGEAN CITIES

The Mycenaean Greeks who conquered King Priam's Troy soon lost their homelands. Power changes forced successive waves of immigration: the Ionians and others settled on the Turkish shore. While Greece went into a 'Dark Age', civilisation blossomed here. By the 8th

THE CRESCENT MOON

Philip of Macedon launched his raid on Byzantium in the dead of night. But the goddess of the moon, Hecate, illuminated the scene and foiled Philip's plot. This divine intervention was commemorated by the striking of coins bearing her star and crescent. Some say that is why the crescent moon became an important symbol, later passed on to the Ottomans and, subsequently, to the Islamic world.

century BC the 12 main city-states of Ionia, including Ephesus, Priene and Miletus, had formed what was known as the Pan-Ionic League. Science, philosophy, architecture and the arts flourished, and the Ionians founded further colonies.

In the 6th century BC coastal city-states fell to the Persians, who incorporated them into their empire. Athens supported a revolt, which was quickly subdued. Athenian involvement provoked the Persian King Darius to invade the Greek mainland. He suffered a succession of defeats: the famous Battle of Marathon in 490BC and the loss of the Persian fleet at the Battle of Salamis 10 years later.

As a result of the Persian Wars, cities along the Aegean coast were encouraged to join the Delian Confederacy, paying tribute to Athens in return for protection against the Persians. Athens demanded this source of easy money and dissent soon grew among the member cities. There followed the Peloponnesian War (431–404BC), after which Sparta led the confederacy. The Persians, sensing weakness in the ranks, launched another offensive, resulting in the Aegean coastal cities coming under Persian control in 387BC.

ALEXANDER THE GREAT

Meanwhile, King Philip II of Macedon dreamed of driving the Persians out of northern Greece and unifying the entire Greek world. He thought Byzantium was well positioned and attempted to take it in 340BC.

Philip's dreams were surpassed by his son, Alexander the Great, who lived for only 33 years (356–323BC). In 334BC, aged 22, he led his army across the Hellespont (now the Dardanelles). He paused at Troy to make a sacrifice at the Temple of Athena and pay homage to his hero Achilles, before going on to defeat the Persians. Having conquered the Aegean and Mediterranean coasts of Anatolia, and subdued Syria and Egypt, Alexander took the great prize of Persepolis, the Persian capital, before advancing into India. He built the greatest empire the world had yet seen, although it lasted only 10 years.

After Alexander's death, his empire was divided among his generals. The conflict between them left the Turkish Aegean and Byzantium open to acquisition by Rome.

ENTER THE ROMANS

Attalus III, the last of the Attalid kings, a dynasty dating from 264BC, ruled a prosperous city-state, Pergamon, on the Aegean. When he died in 133BC, his subjects discovered that he had bequeathed his kingdom to the Romans. Thus Pergamon became the capital of the new Roman province of Asia. Under Emperor Augustus, Rome ceased to be a republic, and, in 27BC, became an empire. There followed a long period of peace and prosperity known as the Pax Romana. Asia Minor (the Roman name for Anatolia) was incorporated into the Roman Empire.

The advent of Christianity threatened the Roman establishment because it rejected the old gods and denied the divinity of the emperor.

The journeys of St Paul the Apostle (AD40–56) led to the founding of numerous churches, notably the Seven Churches of Asia addressed in the Revelation of St John – Pergamon, Smyrna, Ephesus, Thyatira, Laodicea, Sardis and Philadelphia.

CITY OF CONSTANTINE

Meanwhile Byzantium had developed as a city-state, much like the cities of the Aegean. It, too, fell under the sway of Athens, Sparta, Persia, Alexander and Rome. It tried to regain its independence from Rome, but proved too small and weak, and was conquered by Emperor Septimius Severus in AD196. He had the city razed to the ground, but then saw the advantages of its strategic location, and began a programme of enlarging and strengthening the old defensive walls.

Weak and decadent emperors saw the Roman Empire decline into anarchy. In AD286 Diocletian sought to reverse the decline by splitting the administration of the empire in two. His policy succeeded for a time, but following his abdication in AD305, the empire continued to weaken, harassed by invaders and troubled by internal strife.

Theodosian Walls

Constantine the Great (who was a convert to Christianity) reunited the empire. He chose Byzantium as his new capital to emphasise the break with heathen Rome. The city was inaugurated with great ceremony in AD330 and, in honour of the emperor, was renamed Constantinople. Constantine added new city walls, following a plan he claimed to have been given by Christ in a vision, and commissioned many

Hagia Sophia mosaic

monuments, including a grand central forum decorated with a triumphal column. The 'New Rome' soon achieved a pre-eminence in the Christian world it would retain for 1,000 years.

In 392 the Emperor Theodosius proclaimed Christianity to be the official religion of the Roman Empire. On his death in 395 the empire was split once more, between his two sons. The Western Empire, ruled from Rome, fell in 476, but the Eastern, or Byzantine Empire, became one of the longest-lived empires the world has ever known, lasting from 395 to 1453. The greatest of the Byzantine emperors was Justinian (527–65), who extended the boundaries of the empire into Spain, Italy and Africa. Together with his wife, Theodora, he encouraged the arts, reformed the legal system, and commissioned the building of the magnificent basilica, the Hagia Sophia (Aya Sofya).

CRUSADES

Following the death of the Prophet Mohammed in 632, Arab armies, united under Islam, took Egypt, Syria and Palestine from the Byzantines; Constantinople was besieged from 674 to 678, but survived because of its defences. Christian holy places were threatened and pilgrims bound for Jerusalem attacked.

In response, the First Crusade rampaged across the region and finally captured Jerusalem in 1099. However, the Second and Third Crusades were a disaster for the Christians. The Fourth Crusade, launched in 1202 and partly inspired by Venetian jealousy of Byzantium's trading power, became an excuse to plunder Constantinople itself. Thus, the city that had held out against so many attacks by the infidel became subjected to mindless pillaging by fellow Christians. Constantinople was recaptured in 1261, but the city had been shattered and its great monuments were stripped of gold, silver and precious works of art.

Crusaders sack Constantinople

OTTOMAN RULE

The Turks in Anatolia rallied under the banner of Sultan Osman Gazi, and in the 15th century, the whole of Anatolia and Thrace, except for Constantinople, was under the control of the Ottoman Turks. The young Ottoman Sultan, Mehmet II, who reigned from 1451 to 1481, set about cutting off Constantinople's supply lines.

In April 1453 the Sultan's armies massed outside the walls, outnumbering the Byzantines 10 to one. The siege lasted seven weeks. The final assault came on 29 May 1453, when the Ottoman army surged through a breach in the walls. The last emperor, Constantine XI, fell in the fighting, and by noon that day Mehmet II and his men had taken control of the city.

Mehmet II became known as 'Fatih' (Conqueror), and his newly won capital was renamed Istanbul. Mehmet ordered that Hagia Sophia be converted into a mosque; on the following Friday, he attended the first Muslim prayers in what came to be called Aya Sofya Camii (Mosque of Aya Sofya).

During the reign of Mehmet's great-grandson, Süleyman the Magnificent (r.1520–66), the Ottoman Empire reached its greatest and most celebrated heights. The new rulers ornamented Istanbul with elegant, richly decorated buildings, mosques and palaces, public buildings, and fountains. This was the period of the master architect Sinan, whose most famous work is Süleymaniye Mosque.

Süleyman the Magnificent

By the mid-17th century, the Ottoman Empire stretched from the eastern end of the Black Sea to Algeria, taking in Mesopotamia, Palestine, the shores of the Red Sea (including Mecca and Medina), Egypt, Anatolia,

SINAN

Sinan (1489–1588) was the most celebrated Ottoman architect. Before taking up the profession (at the age of 49), he worked as a construction officer in the Janissary corps of the army. He designed hundreds of buildings, but is best remembered for his mosques, which include the Sehzade and Süleymaniye mosques in Istanbul and the Selimiye Mosque in Edirne. He refined the use of domes, half-domes and buttresses both to maximise interior space and to achieve the best natural lighting on the richly decorated interior surfaces.

Greece, the Balkans, Hungary, Moldavia, the North African coast, the Crimea and southern Ukraine..

DECLINE AND FALL

Such far-flung territories made effective rule impossible, and years of decadence, infighting and intermittent wars caused the sultanate to fall into irreversible decline. The failure of the siege of Vienna in 1683 highlighted the weakening. Gradually the sultans moved further and further into European control, bringing in foreigners to advise on, then run, every aspect of the empire.

By the 19th century, Ottoman garb was replaced by Prussian blue uniforms, and the Ottoman Topkapı was replaced by the rococo Dolmabahçe Palace. But attempts at reform came too late; by 1876 the government was bankrupt. Sultan Abdül Hamid II (1876–1909) tried to apply absolute rule, and succeeded only in creating discontent among a younger generation of educated Turks who were increasingly interested in Western ways of government and social organisation; they formed an underground group known as the 'Young Turks'. In 1909, their revolt removed Abdül Hamid and replaced him with his brother, Mehmet V.

There followed the Balkan Wars, and World War I, which Turkey entered on Germany's side. In the Gallipoli campaign of 1915, the

Turks, led by General Mustafa Kemal, defeated the Allied attack on the Dardanelles. At the end of the war, the Treaty of Sèvres stripped the Ottoman Empire of its lands, which were divided between the Allied powers.

ATATÜRK AND THE TURKISH REPUBLIC

In 1920, Mustafa Kemal (Atatürk, see box) was elected president of the Grand National Assembly in Ankara in defiance of the Sultan's government in Constantinople. A war leader and popular politician, he ruthlessly liberated Turkey of foreign invaders and its more independently minded people, such as Armenians. He had the task of abolishing the sultanate without antagonising religious elements (the Sultan was also the caliph, leader of the Islamic world). In 1922, Mehmet VI, last of the Ottoman sultans, finally went into exile.

Atatürk

From 1925 to 1935, Atatürk transformed the country. He secularised institutions, reformed the calendar, adapted the Latin alphabet for the Turkish language, emancipated women, outlawed Dervishes and improved industry and agriculture. He was enormously popular with the common people, and after he died in 1938, thousands lined the railway track to salute the presidential train as it carried him from Istanbul for burial in Ankara, which in 1923 had been made the capital of Turkey. Istanbul lost revenues and status, and the city was left with an uncertain future.

ISTANBUL AT LAST

The 1930s were the romantic 'Orient Express' years celebrated by foreign writers at the Pera Palas Hotel, but the subsequent decade was depressing, blighted by corruption and depopulation.

Since the war, Turkey has had mixed fortunes both economically and politically, with the military often on hand to safeguard Atatürk's legacy from economic and social disorder and from militant Islamist forces. But Istanbul has ploughed on regardless, and since the 1960s, when major transport and restoration schemes were set in motion, its revival has been spectacular. The city has re-established itself as the hub of the nation's cultural life and the powerhouse of its economy, with the largest companies and banks, the main national newspapers, television networks and advertising agencies all having headquarters here.

Clean and efficiently run, Istanbul is back in the top league of world cities, and certainly won't be bowed by the terrorist attacks to which it periodically falls victim. Especially since becoming European Capital of Culture in 2010, Istanbul's profile has risen immensely in the field of tourism and the arts, and with a booming economy. However, the 21st century has also been marked by a lurch towards conservatism from the government, rowing back on certain secularising and progressive policies. The Kariye Museum and Hagia Sophia have been reinstated as mosques, and the Istanbul Pride event has been violently suppressed since 2015.

NOTES

Mustafa Kemal introduced the Western idea of surnames (Turks had previously had a single name). Everyone had to choose a family name, which was handed down to their children. For himself, he chose Atatürk, Father of the Turks: an appropriate name given he single-handedly created the modern Turkish state.

CHRONOLOGY

c.660BC Byzantium founded by Byzas the Greek.

330 Constantine makes Byzantium the new capital of his empire.

395 Death of Theodosius I; final division of Roman Empire.

532–37 Construction of Hagia Sophia (Aya Sofya).

726–843 Iconoclastic Crisis divides the empire.

11th century Seljuk Turks invade Asia Minor.

1204–61 Crusaders sack Constantinople and occupy the city.

1453 Mehmet II (Mehmet the Conqueror) captures Constantinople and makes it his capital, renamed Istanbul.

1520–66 Reign of Süleyman the Magnificent.

1683 Ottoman Empire reaches its greatest extent.

18th century Ottomans lose territory to European powers.

1909 Young Turks depose Sultan Abdül Hamid II.

1915 The Turks under Atatürk defeat Allied attack on the Dardanelles.

1922 The sultanate is abolished.

1923 Turkey becomes a republic; Atatürk elected president.

1952 Turkey joins NATO.

1999 Huge earthquake hits the Istanbul area, killing around 20,000.

2003 Erdogan becomes prime minister.

2005 Negotiations on joining the EU begin.

The Turkish flag inside the courtyard of the Blue Mosque

President Recep Tayyip Erdogan

2010 Istanbul is European Capital of Culture.

2013 Police attacks protesters at Gezi Park; 11 people are killed and more than 8,000 wounded.

2014 Recep Tayyip Erdoğan becomes Turkey's president.

2015 Erdoğan's AKP Party regains its parliamentary majority in a snap election.

2018 Saudi journalist Jamal Khashoggi is murdered in the Saudi consulate in Istanbul.

2023 Istanbul is declared the world's most-visited city by Euromonitor International.

2024 Dozens die in a fire at The Masquerade nightclub in Istanbul. Turkey announces its initiative to map marine parks in the Aegean Sea, a move seen as retaliatory against Greece.

2025 New metro lines in Istanbul due for completion.

Sightseeing ships in Istanbul

Places

Modern Istanbul is split in two by the narrow, sinuous strait known as the Haliç (Golden Horn), an estuary of the Bosphorus. The city mood varies: Sultanahmet, the heart of the Old City, has distinctive architecture – this is where the city's Ottoman history is most keenly felt. Towards the city walls, Fatih is conservative and poorer; Balat and Fener, although run-down, hold treasures of Istanbul's Greek, Armenian and Jewish history. Across the Galata Bridge, the feeling is more cosmopolitan, but with hints of a naughty, *fin-de-siècle*, Art Nouveau history. Taksim Square is much like any main city square, full of traffic and people in a hurry; Beyoğlu is the hip, bohemian area with nightlife and entertainment aplenty. The Asian side of the city, as a general rule, feels more modern, organised and residential.

This guide takes Eminönü as the starting point for tours of Istanbul. It is possible to reach almost all the attractions from this point using public transport. Eminönü is the terminus for the *feribot* (ferries); nearby Sirkeci Station is the European railway terminus, where the Orient Express used to steam in, trailing romance. Travellers today are mostly suburban commuters, and there is a good restaurant and a small museum detailing its romantic past. (Asian trains leave from the Haydarpaşa Station across the Bosphorus.)

NOTES

A sleek tram runs past the Dolmabahçe to Eminönü, across the Galata Bridge, through Sultanahmet, past the Grand Bazaar, the hotels of Laleli and Aksaray, and on to the city walls at Topkapı bus station (not to be confused with the famous palace of the same name). It is a handy way of getting from one sight to another.

THE OLD CITY (STAMBOUL)

HIGHLIGHTS

- Eminönü, see page 34
- Sultanahmet, see page 35

- Hagia Sophia, see page 36
- Topkapı Palace (Topkapı Sarayı), see page 42
- Archaeological Museums, see page 46

EMINÖNÜ

Istanbul's most popular tourist attractions are concentrated in the Sultanahmet district, but before setting out there are sights to be seen in **Eminönü**. At rush hour the waterfront becomes overtaken with bedlam as commuters pour off the ferries from the modern, European side or from the Asian side. The air is loud with blasts from ships' horns, and the water boils white as vessels jostle for a vacant berth. Smaller boats equipped with stoves and frying pans bounce around in the wash, while their crews, seemingly oblivious to the violent, churning movement of their floating kitchens, dish up fried-fish sandwiches to hungry local people standing on the quayside. Adding to the activity, and competing for passing trade, are the vendors with carts from which they sell grilled corn cobs, pickles and fried mussels.

Inside the Spice Bazaar

The wide square opposite Galata Bridge is dominated by the **New Mosque** *(Yeni Camii)*. Commissioned in 1597 by the Valide Sultan Safiye, mother of Mehmet III, it was not completed

THE SPICE OF LIFE

At the Spice Bazaar in Eminönü, sellers once sat cross-legged on carpets, ready to seize pestle and mortar for pounding potions both efficacious and fanciful, optimistically prepared to cure anything from lumbago to lovesickness through to highly complicated cases of combating the Evil Eye. Some of these time-honoured herbal remedies are still available, although you'll no longer find those containing such rare ingredients as ambergris, dragon's blood or tortoise eggs.

until 1663, making the Yeni Camii the youngest of Istanbul's classical mosques.

The large archway to the right of the mosque is the entrance to the famous **Spice Bazaar** ❶ (free) also known as the Egyptian Bazaar *(Mısır Çarşısı)*. It was opened a few years before Yeni Camii, and its revenues originally paid for repairs to the mosque complex. Inside, the L-shaped building has an array of shops, its air heady with aromas of ginger, pepper and cinnamon, although these days it is dominated by tourist-friendly souvenirs, jewellery and fabrics, plus plenty of apple tea and *lokum* (Turkish Delight). The dried fruits, cheese and fresh produce in the stalls outside are far better quality. Nearby streets are filled with local people shopping for household items.

If you leave the Spice Bazaar by the gate at the far end of the first aisle and then turn right, you will find **Rüstem Paşa Mosque** ❷ *(Rüstempaşa Camii; free)*, with its minaret soaring above the narrow backstreet. This is one of Sinan's smaller works, and one of his most beautiful. The interior is almost completely covered in İznik tiles of the finest period, with floral and geometric designs in blue, turquoise and coral red.

SULTANAHMET

The summit of the first of the Old City's seven hills is occupied by **Sultanahmet**. This was the site of the original Byzantium, founded in the 7th century BC, and of the civic centre of Constantinople, capital of the Byzantine Empire. Here, too, the conquering Ottoman sultans chose to build their most magnificent palaces and mosques.

HAGIA SOPHIA

Of the few remains of the Byzantine city, the most remarkable building is **Hagia Sophia** ❸ (also known as Aya Sofya; https://muze.gen.tr/muze-detay/ayasofya; charge). For almost 1,000 years, this was the greatest church in Christendom, an architectural wonder built by the Byzantine Empire to impress the world.

It is thought that a Christian Basilica was built here in AD325 by Emperor Constantine, on the site of a pagan temple. It was

Sultanahmet at night

destroyed by fire in AD404 and rebuilt by Theodosius II, then burnt down again in 532. The building you see today was commissioned by Justinian and completed in 537, although many repairs, additions and alterations have been made over the centuries. The dome was damaged by earthquakes several times, and the supporting buttresses have coarsened the church's outward appearance.

NOTES

One of Hagia Sophia's more curious features is the Weeping Column (Column of St Gregory), which has a thumb-sized hole covered with a brass plate. If you insert your thumb and turn it 360° and it produces moisture, your wishes, allegedly, come true. The water is said to be beneficial for eye diseases.

The finest materials were used in its construction – white marble from the islands of the Marmara, *verd antique* from Thessaly, yellow marble from Africa, gold and silver from Ephesus, and ancient red porphyry columns that possibly came from Egypt and may once have stood in the Temple of the Sun at Baalbek. The interior was covered with golden mosaics, lit by countless flickering candelabras.

The last Christian service ever to be held in Hagia Sophia took place on 28 May 1453, the day before Constantinople fell to the Turks. Mehmet the Conqueror immediately

The cavernous interior

converted the building to an imperial mosque, and built a brick minaret at the south-east corner. The architect, Sinan, strengthened the buttresses and added the other three minarets during the 16th century. Hagia Sophia served as a mosque until 1935, when Atatürk proclaimed that it should become a museum.

In 2020, in the ultimate symbol of the Turkish government's move away from secularisation, Hagia Sophia ceased to be a museum and was reinstated as a working mosque. For a few years, entry was free to all, but this resulted in the building being overwhelmed with visitors, and so in 2024 dramatic changes were made to the way in which visitors access Hagia Sophia. For all visitors, there is now a steep entrance fee. Turkish visitors can access the ground floor as before, but foreign visitors go in through a separate entrance and are limited to the upper gallery (reached by a spiral ramp that starts at the north end of the narthex) and the southwest vestibule, where some of the structure's finest mosaics can be found.

The upper gallery also provides fine views of the building's interior as a whole – note the beautiful matching panels of marble, the vaulted gold mosaic ceiling, and the huge bronze doors of the Imperial Gate. Sooner or later, though, all eyes are drawn skywards by the upwards sweep of the dome. The scale is overwhelming: the

WHERE TO SHOOT THE BEST PICTURES

Hagia Sophia is the principal Byzantine building still standing in Istanbul and one of the finest architectural creations in the world, not least because of its stunning and hugely innovative dome. Sultanahmet Arkeolojik Park provides the best views of the Hagia Sophia; use the terrain in front of you to your advantage for the best shots.

The city's **Blue Mosque** is a delight to photograph, with its cascading domes and slender minarets dominating the skyline, as well as beautiful blue tiles inside. The best shots are from the end of Sultanahmet Arkeolojik Park (near Hagia Sophia), with the fountains in the foreground.

Set atop the most visible hill in Istanbul, the turreted **Topkapı Palace** encompasses a compound of courtyards and pavilions, plus a Byzantine church and Gülhane Park (the only major green and open space in the congested old city). For another great photo op, just beyond the palace, fronting the ferry-filled waters of the Golden Horn, is the fragrant **Spice Bazaar**.

The 61-metre (200ft) -high medieval **Galata Tower** is one of the best places to photograph Istanbul's sweeping rooftop views. Early is the best time because of the steady stream of traffic going around Galata each day.

With some 4,000 shops in a mall over 500 years old, the **Grand Bazaar** is a photography experience few visitors will want to miss. The size of a city street block, the Grand Bazaar has endless rows of storefronts and a staggering variety of merchandise that make for an assault on the senses – and a gift for the camera.

Pamukkale translates as 'cotton castle' and is about as magical as it sounds. Located in the Denizli Province, white petrified waterfalls have been formed by layers of calcium carbonate, creating an otherworldly landscape that's ripe with photography opportunities.

Situate yourself at **Kusadasi Harbour** for a shot over the 350m (1,050ft) causeway connecting Kuşadası to **Güvercin Adası** (Pigeon Island) and Greek mountains behind. Sunsets are notoriously fiery here.

TOPKAPI – THE FILM

Fans of 'exotic' locales will appreciate Jules Dassin's *Topkapı* (1964). The film has some wonderful scenes of Istanbul, including the old wooden houses that used to be such a feature of the city – and some of which still stand, in various states of repair – around Topkapı Palace. The star was Dassin's wife, Melina Mercouri. In the film, she gets her boyfriend (Maximillian Schell) to assemble a team to pull off a heist – stealing the emerald-encrusted Topkapı dagger. The action is terrific, and there's a lengthy sequence featuring the traditional Turkish sport of oil wrestling. The film is enhanced by the presence of Peter Ustinov, who won an Oscar for his performance as a bumbling Brit, and Akim Tamiroff, as a foul-mouthed, drunken cook.

dome is around 31m (100ft) in diameter, and floats 55m (180ft) above the floor – the same height as a 15-storey building.

The sensation of space is created by the absence of supporting walls beneath the dome. It was the great achievement of the architects Isidorus and Anthemius to transfer the weight of the dome to the pillars using semi-domes, arches and pendentives to create the illusion of an unsupported dome.

Eight huge medallions ('calligraphic roundels') bear the Arabic names of Allah, Mohammed, two of his grandsons and the first four caliphs, and a quotation from the Koran in the crown of the dome. These are remnants of Hagia Sophia's 500 years of service as an imperial mosque, as are the elaborate *mihrab* and *mimber* in the apse.

A few Christian **mosaics** survive – above the apse is the Virgin with the infant Jesus, with the Archangel Gabriel to the right. The best mosaics are in the galleries. By the south wall is the famous **Deesis**, an extraordinary 13th-century mosaic showing Christ flanked by the Virgin Mary and St John the Baptist. On the east wall are two images showing Byzantine emperors and empresses making offerings to Christ on his throne (to the left) and to the Virgin and Child.

At the east end of the galleries, two small columns and a circle of green marble mark the spot where the empress sat during services; on the floor of the nave below, a circle of coloured stone, right of centre, is the **Opus Alexandrinum**, the place where the Byzantine emperors were crowned.

As it is a working mosque, there are also new rules on dress codes while visiting Hagia Sophia, notably that women have to cover their hair; headscarves can be purchased at the entrance if you forget one. Another consequence of the building's new status as a place of worship is that professional guides are no longer allowed to give tours inside the building. Instead, you can scan a QR code which takes you to a free online audio tour (headsets are available to rent, but you can use your own headphones).

Across from the entrance of Hagia Sophia is **Hürrem Sultan Hamamı** (www.hurremsultanhamami.com; charge), also known as Roxelana's Bath, a bathhouse built by Mimar Sinan in 1556 for Roxelana, favourite wife of Süleyman the Magnificent.

TOPKAPI PALACE (TOPKAPI SARAYI)

Between Hagia Sophia and the tip of Saray Burnu is

Tower of Justice

the walled enclosure of **Topkapı Palace** ❹ (https://muze.gen.tr/muze-detay/topkapi; charge; included in the Istanbul Museum Pass https://muze.gen.tr/MuseumPasses), the former residence and seat of government of the Ottoman sultans. Begun in 1462 by Mehmet the Conqueror, it was extended by each succeeding sultan until it became a miniature city, which included mosques, libraries, stables, kitchens, schools, the imperial mint, treasuries, barracks, armouries, government offices and audience halls. At its height it supported a population of nearly 4,000.

Sultan Abdül Mecit moved into the newly built Dolmabahçe Palace in 1853 (see page 70), and by 1909 Topkapı was completely abandoned. In 1924 it was converted into a museum, and has been undergoing a continuous programme of restoration ever since. It is the city's most popular tourist attraction, and deserves at least several hours to do it justice. If pushed for time, the essentials are, in order of importance, the Harem (get there early), the Treasury and the Pavilion of the Holy Mantle.

FORBIDDEN FRUITS

The harem occupies an important place in Western fantasy. In fact, the word is derived from the Arabic *haram*, meaning forbidden, and it was the place where the sultan and the women lived. Many women in the Islamic world, especially wives and mothers, had power and influence over their menfolk, but the harem women included 'odalisques', the slave girls who gripped the imagination of writers and artists from Mozart and Balzac to Renoir and Picasso. Many famous artists produced paintings of girls they imagined, but there is little reality in the image. While Matisse was painting his odalisques, Atatürk was proclaiming the Turkish women's right to vote (eventually passed in 1934). When Picasso inherited the fascination from Matisse and began to paint odalisques, Turkish women had equal rights in many areas, including education, and had had the franchise for 30 years.

The palace is laid out as a series of courtyards linked by ceremonial gates. You enter through the **Imperial Gate** (built in 1478) into the wooded gardens of the First Court. On the left is the Byzantine church of **Hagia Eirene** (Divine Peace), rebuilt together with Hagia Sophia after being burnt down in 532. This area was also known as the **Court of the Janissaries**, after the crack military corps that served as the sultan's bodyguard and used it as an assembly ground (the name derives from the Turkish *yeni çeri*, meaning 'new army'). It originally contained the palace bakery, the armoury and the mint. In the far right-hand corner is the ticket office, which originally served as a prison. The fountain is called the Executioner's Fountain because here he rinsed his sword and washed his hands after carrying out his orders; examples of his handiwork were displayed on pikes at the Imperial Gate.

Doorway into the Harem of the Topkapı Palace

Pass through the turreted Gate of Salutations *(Babüsselam)*, better known as the Orta Kapı, or **Middle Gate**. Only the sultan was permitted to ride through this gate on horseback; all others had to dismount and bow. It leads into the Second Court, also known as the **Court of the Divan** because the Imperial Council (the Divan) governed the Ottoman Empire from here. Five avenues radiate from the inside of the gate. To the right lie the **Palace Kitchens**, housing a collection of European crystal, Chinese porcelain, and Ottoman serving dishes and cooking implements. Straight ahead is the ornate Gate of the White Eunuchs *(Babüssaade)*, which leads into the Third Court. The avenue on the left leads towards the pointed **Tower of Justice** *(Adalet Kulesi)*, at the foot of which lie the Council Chamber and the Grand Vezir's Office.

Here, too, is the entrance to Topkapı's main attraction, the **Harem**. The Harem housed the private quarters of the sultan, his mother and his wives and concubines. Its network of staircases, corridors and courtyards linked the sumptuously decorated chambers of the royal household, and harboured a claustrophobic world of ambition, jealousy and intrigue. You enter by the **Carriage Gate**, where the women mounted their carriages. The only adult males allowed in the Harem were the Black Eunuchs, who were in charge of security and administration. Their quarters opened off the narrow **Courtyard of the Black Eunuchs**, beyond the gate. Windows in the colonnade on the left give a glimpse of their tiny rooms; sticks hanging on the walls were used to beat miscreants on the soles of their feet.

The Archaeological Museum

A long, narrow corridor lined with shelves (for trays of food) leads to the Courtyard of the Women Servants, from which you enter the **Apartments of the Valide Sultan** (the sultan's mother, the most powerful woman in the Harem). Her domed sitting room is panelled with 17th-century Kütahya tiles, and decorated with scenic views. A raised platform framed by two columns contains divans and a low dining table. The door on the left, beyond the hearth, leads to the valide sultan's bedchamber, with a gilded bed canopy and ornate floral faïence in turquoise, blue and red. A small adjoining prayer room has scenes of Mecca and Medina.

NOTES

The Persian emperor, Nadir Shah, sent the Ottoman emperor a jewelled throne. To return the compliment, Istanbul dispatched the Topkapı dagger. But en route to Persia, the emissaries discovered that Nadir Shah had died, so they sensibly decided to hang onto the dagger and take it back home with them.

The right-hand door leads to the **Apartments of the Sultan** himself. First you pass the entrance to the royal bath chambers, designed by Sinan and richly ornamented in marble. There are paired but separate chambers for the sultan and the valide sultan, each having a changing room, a cool room and a hot room. The sultan was bathed by elderly female servants, then dried and pampered by groups of younger handmaidens.

Next, you enter the vast and splendid **Imperial Hall**, with three marble fountains, and a canopied throne from which the sultan would enjoy the music and dancing of his concubines. The even more splendid **Salon of Murat III** has inlaid floors, flowered İznik tiles, carved fountains, canopied sofas and a superb domed ceiling, designed by Sinan. On the far side, a door leads to the Library of Ahmet I, with cupboard doors and shutters inlaid with mother-of-pearl and tortoiseshell, which in turn opens into the dining room of Ahmet III, better known as the **Fruit Room**. This tiny room is covered all over with lacquered paintings of flowers and fruit in rococo style. Ahmet III was known as the 'Tulip King', and celebrated each spring with a tulip festival in the palace grounds.

The exit from the Harem opens into the **Third Court**, otherwise reached through the Gate of the White Eunuchs. Inside the gate is the ornate **Throne Room** *(Arz Odası)*, where the sultan received foreign ambassadors. Head down to the right to the **Treasury**, which contains an astonishing selection of artefacts and relics, chief among them the golden Topkapı Dagger, with three huge emeralds set in the hilt and a fourth forming the lid of a watch hidden in the handle; and the Spoonmaker's Diamond, an 86-carat, pear-shaped diamond set in a gold mount encrusted with 49 smaller diamonds. Exhibits include gilded thrones studded with precious stones, a pair of solid-gold candlesticks set with 666 diamonds (one for each verse of the Koran), and reliquaries containing the hand and part of the skull of John the Baptist.

Egyptian Obelisk

Across the courtyard is the magnificently decorated **Pavilion of the Holy Mantle**, which houses relics of the Prophet Mohammed (including hairs from his beard) and is therefore a place of great religious importance for Muslims. The **Fourth Court** contains a number of pretty pavilions and terraces, and a restaurant and cafeteria with fine views of the Bosphorus.

ARCHAEOLOGICAL MUSEUMS

Leaving the palace, a steep, narrow cobbled lane with well-restored Ottoman houses leads to the Fifth Court, which contains these excellent museums (Tue–Sun 9am–7pm, Nov–Mar till 5pm; single charge for all three; another entry by Gülhane tram stop). The **Archaeological Museum** ❺ *(Arkeoloji Müzesi; charge;* https://muze.gov.tr) is made up of three sections, housing one of the world's great collections, with galleries devoted to Cyprus, Syria and Palestine, the Phrygians, Troy and Anatolia, from the Palaeolithic to the Iron Age, as well as the classical era. Its main attraction is the magnificent collection of sarcophagi from Sidon (in modern Lebanon), especially the Alexander Sarcophagus, decorated with scenes of hunting and battle.

The **Museum of the Ancient Orient** *(Eski Şark Eserleri Müzesi)* displays objects from ancient Near and Middle Eastern civilisations, including Babylonian ceramic panels from the Ishtar Gates at the time of King Nebuchadnezzar (605–562BC), Hittite stone sphinxes from Hattusaş, the world's earliest known peace treaty, the Treaty of Kadesh, signed between the Hittites and Egyptians in 1269BC, and the oldest recorded set of laws, the Code of Hammurabi (1750BC).

Built in 1472 for Mehmet the Conqueror, and decorated with turquoise and blue tiles, the most eye-catching building in the square is the **Tiled Pavilion** *(Çinili Kösk)*. It houses a valuable display of ceramics going back to Seljuk times.

NOTES

The Empress Theodora first appeared on stage at the Hippodrome as a dancing girl in a circus troupe. But perhaps her biggest role here came in January AD532, when she faced down an ugly riot between the rival Green and Blue political factions, known as the Nika Revolt. Buildings were set on fire and a new emperor proclaimed. As Justinian prepared to flee the city, the indomitable empress exhorted the troops to rally to his defence. Thirty thousand rioters were killed and the empire was saved.

Inside the Blue Mosque

HIPPODROME

HIGHLIGHTS

The long arc that stretches southwest from Hagia Sophia is known as the **Hippodrome** ❻ *(At Meydanı)*, and in Byzantine times that's exactly what it was. Inspired by the Circus Maximus in Rome, it was built in AD203 as a stadium for chariot-racing and other public events. Later it was enlarged by Constantine the Great and could hold an audience of 100,000.

The Hippodrome was the setting for the ceremony that proclaimed Constantinople as the 'New Rome' in AD330, following the division of the Roman Empire, and soon became the civic centre of the Byzantine capital, decorated with imposing monuments and flanked by fine buildings. Unfortunately, it was destroyed when the city was sacked during the Fourth Crusade, and left stripped of its statues and marble seats. In the 17th century its ruins were used as a quarry for the building of the Blue Mosque. Only its outline, a few brick vaults and three fine ancient monuments, survive today.

The north end of the *spina*, or central axis, is marked by an ornate domed ablutions fountain, given to the city by Germany's Kaiser Wilhelm II to commemorate his visit in 1900. At the opposite end rise three remnants of the original Hippodrome. The **Egyptian Obelisk**, brought to Constantinople by Theodosius in AD390, had been commissioned by Pharaoh Thutmose III in the 16th century BC. What you see is only the top third of the original – it broke during shipment. The reliefs on the pedestal show Theodosius and his family in the Hippodrome presiding over the raising of the obelisk. The **Serpentine Column** consists of three intertwined bronze snakes; they originally supported a gold vase, but the snakes' heads and the vase have long

NOTES

A mosque with six minarets is unusual. Apparently, the sultan wanted to outshine Hagia Sophia, but in doing so, he fell foul of those who felt that he was trying to vie with Mecca (which had six), and so he paid for a seventh minaret for Mecca.

since disappeared. It is the oldest Greek monument in Istanbul, commemorating the Greek victory over the Persians at Plataea in 479BC (it was brought here from Delphi by Constantine the Great). A second, deeply eroded stone obelisk is known as the **Column of Constantine Porphyrogenitus**, as an inscription on its base records that the emperor of that name (AD913–59) had it restored and sheathed in gilded bronze plates.

BLUE MOSQUE

The six minarets of the **Blue Mosque** ❼ (https://sultanahmetcami.org/k/15/english; free but donations are appreciated) dominate the skyline of the Hippodrome. Known in Turkish as *Sultanahmet Camii* (Mosque of Sultan Ahmet), it was built between 1609 and 1616 for the Sultan Ahmet I, after which it became the city's principal imperial mosque because of its proximity to Topkapı Palace. To savour the full effect of the architect's skill, enter the courtyard through the gate that opens onto the Hippodrome. As you pass through the portal, the facade sweeps up in front of you in a fine crescendo of domes. (Go out through the door on the left of the courtyard to reach the entrance for visitors, which leads to the mosque proper.)

Once inside you will see how the mosque earned its familiar name. The very air seems to be blue – more than 20,000 turquoise İznik tiles glow gently in the light from the mosque's 260 windows, decorated with lilies, carnations, tulips and roses. Four massive columns support a dome 22m (70ft) in diameter, and 43m (142ft) high at the crown – big, but not quite as big as Hagia Sophia, the design of which obviously influenced the architect. The *mihrab* and *mimber* are of delicately carved white marble, and the ebony window shutters are inlaid with ivory and mother-of-pearl. The painted blue arabesques in the domes and upper walls are restorations; to see the originals, look at the wall beneath the sultan's loge.

The Blue Mosque stands on the site of Constantine's palace, a treasury of 500 halls and 30 chapels. All that remains is the 6th-century mosaic floor, now housed in the Büyük Saray Mozaikleri (Museum of Great Palace Mosaics; https://muze.gov.tr; charge), reached via the **Arasta Bazaar** (www.arastabazaar.com), a small shopping mall of high-quality craft and jewellery shops.

Across from the Hippodrome and the Blue Mosque is the **Museum of Turkish and Islamic Arts** ❽ (*Türk ve İslam Eserleri Müzesi*; https://muze.gen.tr/muze-detay/tiem). The collection, housed in the former palace of Ibrahim Paşa, the son-in-law of Süleyman the Magnificent, includes illuminated Korans, inlaid Koran boxes, carpets, ceramics, and Persian miniatures.

YEREBATAN SARNICI

Across the tram lines from Hagia Sophia lies the entrance to one of Istanbul's more unusual historic sights – the **Basilica Cistern** ❾, also called the Sunken Palace (*Yerebatan Sarnıcı*; https://yerebatan.com). This amazing construction is part of the city's ancient system of underground reservoirs, which was fed by water from the Belgrade Forest. The cistern measures 140m (460ft) by 70m (230ft); its vaulted brick roof is supported by a forest of columns topped by Corinthian capitals, 336 in all, set in 12 rows of 28. It was built under Justinian in 532 and used during the Byzantine era, but forgotten

Yerebatan Sarayı

Inside the Grand Bazaar

thereafter until 1545 when a Frenchman discovered that residents drew water from wells in their homes. He got into the cistern and it was brought back into use as the water supply for Topkapı.

ÇEMBERLITAŞ

Divan Yolu is the street with tramlines leading uphill from Sultanahmet. It was (and still is) the main road leading to the city gates in Byzantine and Ottoman times. Just off the road, on Klodfarer Caddesi, the **Binbirdirek Sarnıcı** (Cistern of 1001 Columns; charge; www.binbirdirek.com.tr) is an even older 4th-century cistern, with 224 columns – not 1001, in spite of its name.

The next tram stop is called **Çemberlitaş** (Hooped Column) after the stone pillar that rises to the right of the road. Also called the **Burnt Column**, it was charred and cracked by a great fire that ravaged the district in 1770 (the iron hoops help to reinforce the column). Constantine erected it in AD330 to mark the city's new status as capital of the Eastern Roman Empire. Parts of the cross and the nails with which Christ was crucified are reputed to be sealed in the column's base.

Built by Sinan, the **Çemberlitaş Hamamı** (*Vezirhan Caddesi*; www.cemberlitashamami.com) is still in use today as a Turkish bath and well worth a visit.

THE GRAND BAZAAR

Behind the Burnt Column rises the Baroque exterior of the **Nuruosmaniye Camii**, dating from 1755. Walk towards it, then turn left through an arched gate into the mosque precinct and follow the crowds into the bustling **Grand Bazaar** ⑩. The *Kapalı Çarşı* (Covered Market; http://kapalicarsi.com.tr) of Istanbul is the world's largest covered bazaar, with more than 4,000 shops, as well as banks, cafés, restaurants, mosques and a post office, crammed together in a grid of 66 narrow streets that total 8km (5 miles) in length. It's all protected from summer sun and winter rain by a multitude of domed and vaulted roofs. Mehmet the Conqueror built the first covered market on this site in 1461. It has been rebuilt several times after destruction by fire and earthquake.

Most of the streets follow a pattern and are well-signposted. From the Nuruosmaniye entrance, stretching towards the **Beyazıt Gate**, is the main street, lined with jewellers' shops. On your right is the entrance to the 16th-century **Sandal Bedesten**, with brick

NOTES

You'll see many shops selling *nazar boncuk* – glass discs with a distinctive pattern of blue, white and black concentric circles, also sold in the form of jewellery, keyrings and general knick-knacks. These are considered a talisman to avert the evil eye and bring good luck.

vaults supported on stone pillars. It is quiet for most of the week, but comes alive during the auctions held here at 1pm on Tuesday, Wednesday and Thursday. In the centre of the bazaar is the **Old Bedesten**, where you can find the best-quality gold and silver jewellery, brass and copper ware, curios and antiques.

The Beyazıt Gate, at the far end of the main street *(Kalpakcılar Başı Caddesi)*, leads to a street of bargain clothing stalls. Turn right, and first left up the steps to the **Book Market** *(Sahaflar Çarşısı)*, a tiny, historic courtyard, popular with students.

BEYAZIT

The next tram stop, **Beyazıt**, brings you to **Beyazıt Meydanı**, a vast, pigeon-thronged square below the entrance to Istanbul

Friday prayers at the Süleymaniye Mosque

University (www.istanbul.edu.tr). Site of the Roman Forum Tauri (Forum of the Bulls), it has been one of the city's main gathering points for 2,000 years. It's a busy square, full of students, children and vendors, as well as many pigeons.

The east side of the square is dominated by the beautiful **Beyazıt Camii**, built in the early 16th century by Sultan Beyazıt II, son of Mehmet the Conqueror. It is the earliest surviving example of classical Ottoman architecture, inspired by Hagia Sophia. Opposite the mosque is the arched gateway to Istanbul University and the 50m (148ft) **Beyazıt Tower**, built in 1828 as a fire-lookout point and still in use. On the west side of the square is the Calligraphy Museum (closed for restoration at time of writing), part of the old *medresse*.

The impressive interior of Süleymaniye Mosque

SÜLEYMANIYE MOSQUE

The outline of the **Mosque of Süleyman the Magnificent** ⓫ *(Suleymaniye Camii;* www.ktb.gov.tr/EN-113783/suleymaniye-mosque.html*; free)*, rises from a site above the Golden Horn (near the north gate of Istanbul University). Deemed the finest Ottoman building in Istanbul, the mosque is a tribute to the 'Golden Age' of the Ottoman Empire, and to the two great men of genius who created it – Sultan Süleyman I and his chief architect, Sinan. Süleyman, known in Turkish as Kanuni (The Lawgiver), reigned from 1520–66, when the empire attained the height of its wealth and power.

Süleymaniye Mosque and its complex of buildings were built between 1550 and 1557. Legend has it that jewels from Persia were ground up and mixed in with the mortar for one of the minarets, and that the incredible acoustics were achieved by embedding 64 hollow clay vessels facing neck-down in the dome. It is also said that Süleyman, in awe of his architect's achievement, handed the keys to Sinan at the inauguration ceremony and allowed him the privilege of opening it.

You enter through a courtyard, colonnaded with grand columns of granite, marble and porphyry, with a rectangular *şadırvan* (ablutions fountain) in the centre. The interior is vast and inspiring,

Valens Aqueduct

flooded with light from the 16th-century stained-glass windows. The mosque is square in plan, about 58m (172ft) on each side, capped by a dome 27.5m (82ft) in diameter and 47m (140ft) high. The tiles are original İznik faïence, with floral designs; the woodwork of the doors and shutters is delicately inlaid with ivory and mother-of-pearl.

Both Süleyman and Sinan are buried nearby. The **tombs** of the sultan and his wife Roxelana lie behind the mosque in the walled garden, where roses and hollyhocks tangle among the tall grass between the gravestones, and sparrows swoop and squabble in the fig trees. Sinan's modest tomb, which he designed himself, stands in a triangular garden just outside the northern corner of the complex, capped by a small dome.

A walk around the terrace beside the mosque, which affords a fine view across the Golden Horn, gives some idea of the size of the complex with its attendant soup kitchen and caravanserai, school and library, now housing restaurants and archives. The **hamam** is back in use.

TOWARDS THE CITY WALLS

The tram continues towards the city walls, passing Laleli and Aksaray, where there are many hotels, and out to the suburbs. There are a number of worthwhile sights between Süleymaniye Mosque and the city walls, but they are scattered and require a long walk or bus or taxi rides. Away from the main roads, these neighbourhoods contain a maze of backstreets, muddy lanes and cobbled alleys. If you choose to walk, there are some good large-scale maps available. The odd, old wooden house that has survived the city's numerous fires leans creaking across the crumbling bricks of some forgotten Byzantine ruin.

One of Sinan's early buildings, in memory of Prince Mehmet, Süleyman the Magnificent's son, who died in 1543 aged 21, is the imposing Mosque of the Prince *(Şehzade Camii)*, overlooking a park that is spoilt by traffic noise.

Byzantine beauty at the Kariye Mosque

AQUEDUCT OF VALENS

Spanning the park and the six lanes of the busy thoroughfare Atatürk Bulvarı are the impressive remains of the **Aqueduct of Valens** *(Bozdoğan Kemeri)*. Constructed in the 2nd century AD, it was rebuilt by Emperor Valens in the 4th century, restored several times by both the Byzantines and the Ottomans, and remained in use up till the 19th century.

If you follow the line of the aqueduct away from the city centre, you soon reach the vast complex of the **Mosque of the Conqueror** *(Fatih Camii)*, perched on top of the city's Fourth Hill. It was the first imperial mosque to be built following the Conquest of Constantinople in 1453, and its *külliye* (mosque complex), the biggest in the whole of the Ottoman Empire, included a hospital, almshouses, a mental asylum, visitors' accommodation and a number of schools teaching science, mathematics, history and Koranic studies. Built by Mehmet the Conqueror between 1462 and 1470, the complex was almost completely destroyed by an earthquake in 1766. Only the courtyard and its huge portal survived; the rest was rebuilt. The tombs of the conqueror and his wife are in the walled graveyard behind the mosque. Wednesday sees a lively street market selling everything from vegetables to umbrellas and underwear.

Farther out, dominating the Fifth Hill, is the **Mosque of Selim I** *(Sultan Selim Camii)*, dedicated to the father of Süleyman the Magnificent. Its dedicatee was known as Yavuz Selim (Selim the Grim), but the mosque is one of the loveliest in the city, with sparse, tasteful decoration of beautiful İznik tiles in turquoise, blue and yellow, and richly painted woodwork. Its dramatic situation overlooking the Golden Horn commands a sweeping view across the picturesque districts of Fener and Balat.

KARIYE MOSQUE

The brightest jewel in Istanbul's Byzantine crown is the former Chora Church, now housing the **Kariye Mosque** ⓬ (*Kariye Cami*; https://muze.gen.tr/muze-detay/kariye; closed to non-Muslim visitors on Friday; charge). Opened as a museum in 1958, this small building, tucked away in a quiet corner, remains one of the world's greatest monuments to Byzantine art after its re-conversion into a working mosque in 2024. The building's new status means the usual mosque dress code applied (no shorts or bare shoulders, and head coverings for women).

The oldest part of the existing building, the central domed area, dates from 1120. The church was rebuilt and decorated early in the 14th century under the supervision of Theodore Metochites, an art-lover, statesman and scholar who was a friend and adviser of Emperor Andronicus II Palaeologus. Sadly, Metochites was reduced to poverty and sent into exile when the emperor was overthrown in 1328. He was allowed to return in 1330 provided he remained a monk at Chora, which he did, living the last years of his life surrounded by the magnificent works of art he had commissioned.

Metochites left the central portion of the church intact, but added the outer narthex and the parecclesion (side chapel). The wonderful mosaics and frescoes, dating from 1310–20, are almost certainly the work of a single artist, now unknown. Their subtlety of colour, liveliness of posture, and strong, lifelike faces record a last flowering of Byzantine art before its descent into decadence. The church was converted into a mosque in 1511, but fortunately it was not substantially altered. The mosaics were covered with wooden screens, some windows were boarded up, and a minaret was added. The 2024 re-conversion has seen most of the mosaics left on display, with those in the nave (which is now the men's prayer area) hung with curtains which cover them during prayer time.

The **mosaics** are grouped into four narrative cycles depicting the lives of Christ and the Virgin Mary, along with portraits of various saints, and large dedicatory panels. The mosaic above the door leading from the narthex into the nave shows the figure of Metochites, wearing a huge hat, offering a model of his beloved church to Christ. Each tiny tile is set at a different angle to its neighbours so that the reflected light creates the illusion of a shimmering, ethereal image. The **frescoes** are all in the parecclesion, which stretches the length of the building and was used in Byzantine times as a funerary chapel. The artist's masterpiece is the *Anastasis* (Resurrection) in the vault of the apse, showing Christ pulling Adam and Eve from their tombs, while the figure of Satan lies bound and helpless beneath his feet.

Fifteen minutes' walk from the museum, and marking the summit of the Sixth Hill, is the **Mihrimah Sultan Camii**, built by Sinan in 1565 for Süleyman's favourite daughter. Next to the mosque are the **Theodosian Walls**, pierced here by the **Adrianople Gate** *(Edirnekapı)* where Mehmet the Conqueror entered the fallen city in 1453. The double walls, built in the 5th century during the reign of Emperor Theodosius, stretch 6.5km (4 miles) from the Sea of Marmara to the Golden Horn. They were defended by 96 towers and had numerous gates. Much of the inner wall and several of the towers are still standing. Seven gates are still in use. It is possible to follow the walls as there are roads alongside them and in some places you can walk on the actual wall. The state of repair varies from section to section, and there is a great deal of painstaking renovation work being carried out.

Inside the Mihrimah Sultan Camii in Üsküdar

YEDIKULE

At the Marmara end of the Theodosian Walls, far from the city's other sights but easily reached by bus or taxi, stands **Yedikule** (Seven Towers; charge). The ancient fortress encloses the **Golden Gate** *(Altınkapı)*, the triumphal arch of the Byzantine emperors, which existed before the walls were built and was incorporated into them. In 1470 Mehmet the Conqueror further strengthened the ancient portal by building three towers of his own, linked by curtain walls to the four Byzantine towers flanking the Golden Gate. During Ottoman times the fortress was used as a prison and a treasury.

Service at Eyüp mosque

EYÜP AND THE GOLDEN HORN (HALIÇ)

HIGHLIGHTS

- The New City (Beyoğlu) , see page 64
- Galata and Pera, see page 65

The **Golden Horn** is an inlet of the Bosphorus, penetrating 7.5km (4.5 miles) into the hills behind the city. It forms a natural harbour, and in Ottoman times was the site of the Imperial Tershane (Naval Arsenal), capable of holding 120 ships. It later became an industrial area, but the factories and shipyards have given way to hotels and tourist attractions. Millions have been spent on improving the water quality.

Hourly ferries depart from the upstream side of Galata Bridge for the half-hour trip along the Golden Horn to the suburb of **Eyüp**, which contains one of Islam's most sacred shrines. **Eyüp Sultan Camii** ⓭ marks the burial place of Eyüp Ensari, the standard-bearer of the Prophet Mohammed. He died in battle while carrying the banner of Islam during the Arab siege of Constantinople (674–8). Following the conquest in 1453, his grave was rediscovered, and Mehmet the Conqueror erected a shrine on the spot, followed in 1458 by a mosque, the first to be built in Istanbul. Thereafter each sultan, on his accession, visited Eyüp Camii to gird himself ceremonially with the Sword of Osman, the first Ottoman sultan. The original mosque was destroyed by an earthquake in 1766; the present building dates from 1800. The **Tomb of Eyüp Ensari**, behind the mosque, is decorated with gold, silver and coloured tiles, and is protected by a gilded grille. Remember that this is a sacred place – dress respectfully and remove shoes before entering (women should cover their legs, upper arms and hair).

Covering the hillside behind the mosque is a vast cemetery littered with turbanned headstones. A path and cable car *(teleferik)* lead up

PIERRE LOTI

Louis Marie Julien Viaud (1859–1923) was a French naval officer whose travels took him to various places in the East and the South Seas. They provided a background for a steady stream of novels, about one per year, written under the pseudonym Pierre Loti. His books were once popular and highly regarded, but are now largely forgotten among English-speaking people.

Aziyadé, part autobiography and part romance, recounts his travels to Constantinople and his love affair with the green-eyed Circassian harem girl, Aziyadé. The book shows a passionate nature, and a man's dreams and melancholy in Constantinople in the last days of the Ottoman Empire. The café at Eyüp is where Pierre Loti is best remembered, but there's an eponymous restaurant and hotel in Sultanahmet.

to the **Pierre Loti Café**, named in honour of the 19th-century French writer who lived in the neighbourhood, and wrote romantic novels about life in Istanbul. The café enjoys a splendid view down the Golden Horn to the distant domes and minarets of Stamboul. The *teleferik* gets busy on summer evenings and at weekends.

A short bus ride from Eyüp is the **Santralistanbul Museum of Energy** (*Silahtar*; www.santralistanbul.org; free except guided tours), a restored Ottoman-era power station, now a superb arts venue with contemporary exhibitions and a restaurant.

On the opposite side of the Golden Horn, at Sutluce, is a children's favourite, **Miniaturk** (*İmrahor Caddesi*; http://miniaturk.com.tr). Its miniature buildings and monuments have been selected to reflect the variety of landmarks in the Ottoman Empire. A little further south (accessible by bus), the **Rahmi M Koç Museum** (*Hasköy Caddesi*; charge; www.koc.com.tr/sustainability/rahmi-koc-museum), housed in an old iron foundry on the south side of the Golden Horn, is a fascinating private collection of scientific, technological and transport items, from an 1898 steam car to a 1940s US submarine as well as masses of smaller instruments, toys and hands-on things to play with. Not the obvious Turkish 'sight' but well worth visiting.

NOTES

On the south side of the Golden Horn, between the ferry stops of Fener and Balat, stands the Church of St Stephen of the Bulgars. This is an unusual building, for the neo-Gothic structure and decorations are made entirely of iron. The sections were cast in Vienna and shipped down the Danube and across the Black Sea. It was built for Istanbul's Bulgarian community in 1871, and is still used for worship.

THE NEW CITY (BEYOĞLU)

The north shore of the Golden Horn was traditionally the quarter where craftsmen, foreign merchants and diplomats made their homes, beginning in the 11th century when the Genoese founded a trading colony in the district of Galata. Following the conquest, European ambassadors built their mansions on the hills beyond Galata, a place which came to be called Pera (Greek for 'beyond'). Foreigners from the entire Ottoman Empire flooded into Galata and Pera, attracted by the wealth and sophistication of the capital. As the area became crowded, the wealthy foreign merchants and diplomats moved farther along the 'Grande Rue de Pera' (now İstiklal Caddesi), forming a focus for the 19th- and 20th-century expansion of the modern, European-style part of Istanbul, known as Beyoğlu.

Galata Tower

GALATA AND PERA

The mouth of the Golden Horn is spanned by the **Galata Bridge** ⓮. The first bridge here was a wooden structure, built in 1845. It was replaced in 1910 by the famous old pontoon bridge with its seafood restaurants, which served until the present one was opened in 1992. The bridge is thronged with fishermen and a waving forest of rods occupies every last piece of space. As you walk across the bridge, your eyes are drawn naturally to the pointed turret of Galata Tower. Sometime during the 11th century, a rough bunch of coastal traders and drifters from every port in the

Mediterranean began to settle on the northern shore of the Horn, in the maritime quarter which became known as Galata.

To avoid the steep climb up the hill beyond Galata Bridge take the **Tünel**, the world's second oldest (and probably shortest) underground railway, built in 1875. The trip to the top station (Tünel) takes just 90 seconds. To reach Galata Tower from here, follow the signs back down the hill.

Galata Tower ⓯ (*Galata Kulesi*; charge) was the keystone in the colony's defences. Its age is uncertain, but it seems to have been built in its present form in 1349, at the highest point of the walls. With an open viewing gallery and restaurant at the top (open till late; belly dancer shows at 8pm, book in advance), it offers fine views over the city, and across the Golden Horn you can count the minarets and domes of Old Istanbul's skyline. Near the tower is modern art research centre SALT Galata (https://saltonline.org/en/42/salt-galata; free), which attracts the local art crowd.

A whirling dervish dancer

Up the hill on Galipdede Caddesi are shops selling books and musical instruments. There's also the **Galata Mevlevihanesi** ⓰, the former Whirling Dervish Hall, where Sufis whirled from 1491 until Atatürk proscribed their practices in 1924. The centre is now the Museum of Divan Literature (https://muze.gen.tr/muze-detay/galatamevlevi; charge), where manuscripts and a selection of instruments are preserved in glass cabinets. Public performances of the order's distinctive whirling, trance-inducing dance, are held on Sundays at 6pm. The centre is also home for a community of cats, who bask on the graves in the peaceful courtyard.

Just up the road, restored 1920s trams clang their way along **İstiklal Caddesi** ⓱ (Avenue of Independence), once lined with the palatial embassies of foreign powers. The mansions have been downgraded to consulates since the capital was transferred to Ankara in 1923, and modern shops and restaurants have sprung up. The street is now pedestrianised, and has some of the city's smartest cafés and many international chain stores. At Galatasaray Square, where İstiklal Caddesi bends to the right, an elegant wrought-iron gateway marks the entrance to the 19th-century **Galatasaray Lisesi**, the Franco-Turkish *lycée* (secondary school) that educated many of the great names in modern Turkish history. Just behind it is another of Istanbul's great historic hamams, the **Tarihi Galatasaray Hamamı** (Turnacıbaşı Sokak 24; www.galatasarayhamami.com).

Past the square on the left is the entrance to **Çiçek Pasajı** (Flower Alley; www.tarihicicekpasaji.com), a high, glass-roofed arcade lined with bars and restaurants. The opposite end of the arcade leads into the **Balık Pazarı** (Fish Market), a block of narrow streets lined with small restaurants and stalls selling fish, fruit and vegetables, and a local speciality snack – *midye tava* (fried mussels on a stick). Go back to Galatasaray Square, and left at the British Consulate along Meşrutiyet Caddesi, and you will reach the beautiful **Pera Palas Hotel** (https://perapalace.com/en). Established in 1892, it provided accommodation for Orient Express passengers and displays highlight its historic ephemera. Agatha Christie stayed in Room 411 when writing *Murder on the Orient Express*. Room 101, the suite used by Atatürk, has been kept as a museum. The old Bristol Hotel is now the **Pera Museum** (Meşrutiyet Caddesi 141; www.peramuzesi.org.tr), housing the Kiraç family collection of

Tram on İstiklal Caddesi

Kutahya tiles and European portraits of life at the Ottoman imperial court. Not far, at İstiklâl Caddesi 136, a 19th-century townhouse has been transformed into the three storey ultra-modern exhibition space **SALT** (www.saltonline.org; charge), with an English-language bookshop and a panoramic restaurant.

TAKSIM AND BEYOND

HIGHLIGHTS

- The Bosphorus Shore, see page 69
- Dolmabahçe Palace, see page 70

Beyond Çiçek Pasajı, the side streets off İstiklal Caddesi are the focus for Istanbul's raunchier nightlife. Buzzing bars and cafés are always springing up here, especially at the Tünel end. Look out for great live music venues from techno to jazz. The street ends at **Taksim Square** *(Taksim Meydanı)*, the heart of modern Istanbul, lined with hotels. The governmental proposal to build a shopping centre on the site of Gezi Park, the only green space in this area, provoked social protests in 2013 and the rise of the movement Occupy Gezi. The **Atatürk Cultural Centre**, once the city's largest concert hall and fine example of modern Turkish architecture, closed in 2008 for renovation and finally re-opened in 2021 (https://akmistanbul.gov.tr/homepage).

At the far end of the square Cumhuriyet Caddesi leads past the Hilton Hotel for a good kilometre (0.75 mile) to the **Military Museum** ⓲ (*Askeri Müzesi*, charge). The exhibits include a section of the massive chain that the Byzantines used to stretch across the mouth of the Golden Horn to keep out enemy ships, as well as captured enemy cannon and military banners, the campaign tents from which the Ottoman sultans controlled their armies, and examples of uniforms, armour and weapons from the earliest days of the empire down to the 20th century. The main attraction is the concert given each afternoon at around 3pm by the **Janissary Band** *(Mehter Takımı)*, a revival of the Ottoman military band that accompanied the sultans' armies on campaigns and led victory processions through the conquered cities. The colourful uniforms are exact replicas of the originals.

Taksim Square also leads to the shopping districts of **Çukurcuma** (southwest) with antiques dealers and cafés and **Teşvikiye** and **Nişantaşı** (north), home of designer labels. Created by famous writer Orhan Pamuk, the **Mazumiyet Müzesi** ⓳ (Museum of Innocence; www.masumiyetmuzesi.org; free), shows Istanbul life as it was in the second half of 20th century.

THE BOSPHORUS SHORE

Karaköy Square *(Karaköy Meydanı)*, at the northern end of the Galata Bridge, is home to the local fish market and is a great place to

Janissary Band member

begin a walk through the old docks area where the cruise-ship terminus is located. A couple of tram stops north-east is **Istanbul Modern** ⓴ (*Meclis-i Mebusan Caddesi Liman Sahası*; www.istanbulmodern.org), housed in a former customs warehouse on Karaköy pier, which has a permanent collection of modern Turkish paintings, sculpture, photography, video and sound installations, as well as a room for touring exhibitions. There is also an art-house cinema and a chic first floor café-bar with superb views.

DOLMABAHÇE PALACE

Take the tram to Kabataş and along to **Dolmabahçe Palace** ㉑ (*Dolmabahçe Sarayı*; www.dolmabahce-palace.com; charge; guided tours only). Sultan Abdül Mecit (reigned 1839–61) decided that Topkapı Palace was too old-fashioned. He commissioned a vast new palace on the shores of the Bosphorus, on the site of a park that had been created by filling in an old harbour (*dolmabahçe* means 'filled-in garden'). Completed in 1853, the palace was intended as a statement of the sultan's faith in the future of his empire, but instead it turned out to be a monument to folly and extravagance. Its construction nearly emptied the imperial treasury, and the running costs contributed to the empire's bankruptcy in 1875.

The guided tour is in two parts – first the **Selamlık** (public rooms) and **Throne Room**, then the **Harem** (private apartments). Highlights of the *Selamlık* include the vast Baccarat and Bohemian crystal chandeliers, 36 in all, and crystal balusters of the main staircase, the sultan's bathroom, two huge bearskins (a gift from the Tsar of Russia), Sèvres vases, Gobelin tapestries and carpets, and the vast bed used by the 'giant sultan', Abdül Aziz. The Throne Room is huge and lavishly decorated.

Further along the waterfront, the **Naval Museum** ㉒ (*Deniz Müzesi*, Iskele Caddesi, Beşiktaş; http://en.besiktas.bel.tr/entry/istanbul-naval-museum) is a reminder that the Ottoman Empire was one of the world's great sea powers. This is a fascinating repository of naval memorabilia, from charts and the personal records, clothes and belongings of Turkish sailors to the splendidly ornate Ottoman royal barges. Outside the museum is the statue and tomb of 16th-century admiral Barbarossa.

Just 2km (1.5 miles) beyond Dolmabahçe you can escape from the city among the wooded walks of **Yıldız Palace and Park** (www.millisaraylar.gov.tr), once the hunting grounds of the sultans. The ornate **Şale Köskü** (Chalet Pavilion; charge), now an interesting little museum, was built by Abdül Hamid II in 1882 for the sultan's

THE END OF A DYNASTY

It is appropriate that Dolmabahçe Palace, the main financial drain that contributed to the downfall of the empire in 1875, was witness to the final act of the empire.

When Atatürk's government abolished the sultanate in November 1922, Mehmet VI, the last representative of the dynasty that had ruled the Ottoman Empire for six centuries, was ignominiously smuggled aboard a British warship anchored off Dolmabahçe, to spend his last years in exile. Atatürk died in the palace on 10 November 1938 at 9.05am, the hour at which all the palace clocks were stopped.

The ornate Dolmabahçe Palace, near Beşiktaş

guests, but the paranoid Abdül Hamid moved in himself until he was deposed in 1909, living a solitary life as a carpenter. Another restored royal pavilion is nearby: **Malta Köskü** has been converted into a café, with a terrace looking over the treetops to the Bosphorus.

ACROSS TO ASIA

You can head from the hustle and bustle of Eminönü or Beşiktas across the water to Asia. **Üsküdar** lies opposite, at the eastern shore of the Bosphorus. The ferry passes **Kız Kulesi** ㉓ (Maiden's Tower), perched on a tiny island about 200m/yds offshore. The name is derived from a legend about a princess confined by her father to protect her from the fate foretold by a dire prophecy: that she would die from the bite of a serpent. Ironically, the princess was eventually bitten by a snake that arrived in one of the baskets containing supplies. Originally a 12th-century Byzantine fort, the present tower dates from the 18th century, and has served as a lighthouse, customs office and control tower. It is now used as a restaurant and café (www.kizkulesi.com.tr) with shuttle boat services from both sides of Istanbul. In Byzantine times a huge chain could be slung between here and the Saray Burnu Peninsula to close the mouth of the Bosphorus. The ferry leaves you at Üsküdar's main square, Iskele Meydanı. Note the **İskele Camii**, designed by Sinan in 1548 for Mihrimah, daughter of Süleyman the Magnificent, and the **Yeni Valide Camii** from the early 18th century. West of the square is Sinan's **Şemşi Paşa Camii** (1580) on the waterfront.

Üsküdar was known as Scutari by Europeans, and Scutari is traditionally associated with the name of Florence Nightingale. During the Crimean War (1854–6) the English nurse set up a hospital in what is now the enormous **Selimiye Barracks** *(Selimiye Kışlası)*, situated in the district of Harem to the south of Üsküdar. A small corner of the building is kept as a **museum** (daily 9am–5pm) in her memory – the exhibits include the famous lamp, which led to her being called 'The lady with the lamp'. Down a lane off Tibbiye Caddesi, the **Commonwealth War Graves Commission Haidar Pasha Cemetery** *(Commonwealth Harp Mezarligi Haidarpaşa)* is a tranquil, beautiful spot. There is a huge memorial to the Crimean War, and the dead from that war (mostly victims of cholera) and the two world wars rest in immaculate graves, with men from the UK and the Indian subcontinent lying side by side.

LOCAL EXCURSIONS

HIGHLIGHTS

- Along the Bosphorus, see page 74
- The Princes' Islands, see page 76
- Belgrade Forest, see page 77
- Black Sea, see page 78

The Maiden's Tower

ALONG THE BOSPHORUS

The **Bosphorus** *(Istanbul Boğazı)* is the narrow strait linking the Black Sea to the Sea of Marmara, and separating the European part of Turkey from the vast hinterland of Anatolia. The winding channel is 30km (18 miles) long and about 2km (1.5 miles) wide, narrowing to 750m (2,450ft) at Rumeli Hisarı.

The strait, once navigated by Jason and the Argonauts in their search for the Golden Fleece, and crossed on a bridge of boats by the Persian army of King Darius in 512BC, en route to battle with the Scythians, is today busy with commercial shipping, ferries and fishing boats. Its wooded shores are lined with pretty fishing villages, old Ottoman mansions, and the villas of Istanbul's wealthier citizens. It is spanned by two impressive suspension bridges. The first bridge to link Europe and Asia was the **Bosphorus Bridge**

(Boğağziçi Köprüsü) at Ortaköy, opened in 1973. It was followed in 1988 by the **Fatih Sultan Mehmet Bridge** at Rumeli Hisarı. Further north construction on the Yavuz Sultan Selim Bridge began in 2013.

The **boat trip up the Bosphorus** ㉔ (many sailings daily from private and public companies) from the pier at Eminönü is worth every penny. The ferry weaves back and forth between Europe and Asia, calling first at Beşiktaş and then a string of attractive villages. You can remain on the boat for the round trip, or stop for lunch at Anadolu Kavağı, or disembark anywhere and return by bus or taxi. Plenty of private companies offer shorter cruises if you are pressed for time; there is also a non-stopping 90-minute evening cruise in summer.

The public ferry heads north, past Istanbul Modern and Çirağan Palace, now a luxury hotel, stopping at Beşiktaş where you can visit Dolmabahçe Palace, the Naval Museum and Yıldız Park. From here you pass beneath the Bosphorus Bridge. Beneath its western end is **Ortaköy**, with a waterfront mosque. The village is a pleasant place, with shops, art galleries, bookstalls and cafés. Just beyond the bridge, on the Asian shore, is **Beylerbeyi Palace** (www.millisaraylar.gov.tr; charge), a sultan's summer residence and hunting lodge built in 1865.

If you continue past the rich suburbs of **Arnavutköy** and **Bebek**, famed for their wonderful *yalıs* (ornate wooden mansions on the waterfront), you will soon reach the massive fortress of **Rumeli Hisarı** (charge). It was built at the command of Mehmet II in 1452 in preparation for his last assault on Constantinople. Its walls enclose a pleasant park with an open-air theatre that occasionally hosts folk-dancing and concerts in summer. On the opposite shore is the smaller and older fortress of **Anadolu Hisarı** (closed to the public), dating from 1390. South of the fort is the ornate rococo facade of the **Küçüksu Pavilion** (*Küçüksu Kasri*; www.ktb.gov.tr/EN-113766/kucuksu-palace.html), an Ottoman summer-house

The sleek Bosphorus Bridge

built on a favourite picnic spot known as the Sweet Waters of Asia.

Beyond the Fatih Sultan Mehmet Bridge the boat stops at **Kanlıca** on the Asian shore, a village famous for its yoghurt, which you can sample at one of the waterside cafés. The upper reaches of the Bosphorus are lined with picturesque fishing villages – **Tarabya**, **Sarıyer** and **Rumeli Kavağı** – where you can enjoy a meal at one of many seafood restaurants. In Sarıyer you can also visit the **Sadberk Hanım Museum** ㉕ (Buyukdere Piyasa Caddesi 27; www.sadberkhanimmuzesi.org.tr/en; charge), a fabulous private collection covering the period from 500BC to Ottoman times, housed in two 19th-century villas. Well-presented displays of gold jewellery, embroidery, costumes and Anatolian figurines help make this one of the finest small museums in Turkey.

Last stop is **Anadolu Kavağı** on the Asian side, a picturesque place overlooked by a Byzantine castle, where the ferry leaves you for a couple of hours or so.

THE PRINCES' ISLANDS

An hour's ferry trip to the southwest of Istanbul lies the bucolic retreat of the **Princes' Islands** ㉖, known to the Turks simply as Adalar, 'The Islands'. This archipelago of nine islands in the Sea of

Marmara has been inhabited since Byzantine times by monastic communities, and was a place of exile for deposed rulers. The Emperor Justin II built a palace on the largest island in the 6th century; it soon came to be known as Prinkipo, the Prince's Isle, and the name later spread to cover the whole group. Today the islands' pretty beaches provide a perfect weekend retreat for the people of Istanbul. Cars are banned, and all transport is by foot, bicycle or *feyton* (horse-drawn carriage).

Check at the ferry terminal for times of ferries, leaving from Eminönü and Beşiktas; also check terminals for inter-island trips. The biggest and most popular island is **Büyükada** (Big Island), with a pleasant town, a picturesque monastery and the modern **Museum of Princes' Islands** (*Adalar Muzesi Hangar*; Aya Nikola Mevkii; charge). You can take a tour of the island on a *fayton* – to find the 'taxi rank', walk uphill from the jetty to the clock tower in the square and turn left. You can also walk to most places, including a steep uphill hike to **St George's Monastery**, where there are iron rings in the marble floor of the chapel that were used to restrain the mentally ill, who were once brought here, hoping to be cured by the waters. There is a simple, delightful restaurant in the monastery's outdoor courtyard. The ferry also calls at the islands of **Kinalıada, Burgazada** and **Heybeliada**, so it's possible to visit two in one day.

BELGRADE FOREST

This is an area north of Istanbul and west of Sarıyer that was once more or less a nature reserve kept for royal hunting. There was a village called Belgrade founded by Süleyman the Magnificent, who moved people from the other Belgrade into the area to look after the reservoirs and aqueducts that provided Istanbul's water, so there are scattered remains of all this activity. Nowadays, people use the forest for picnics and exercise, so it is popular during summer weekends.

NOTES

'There is no difference between the Johnnies and the Mehmets to us, where they lie side by side here in this country of ours. You, the mothers who sent their sons from faraway countries, wipe away your tears; Your sons are now lying in our bosom and are in peace after having lost their life on this land. They have become our sons as well.'

The words of Atatürk on a memorial at Gallipoli

BLACK SEA

There are some small, pleasant resorts accessible from Istanbul, with sandy beaches and clean air. They can be reached by *dolmuş* or minibus. **Kilyos**, about 35km (22 miles) from the centre of Istanbul on the European side, is reached via Sarıyer. The beach (the private stretch is worth paying for) is long but the sea has some dangerous currents. The ruins of a Genoese castle can be seen but not visited as the area is in use by the military; however, there are some good walks. On the Asian side, there's transport from Üsküdar to **Sile**, which takes about an hour. Sile is fairly quiet during the week, but becomes the Brighton of Istanbul at the weekend. It has high cliffs and good fish restaurants.

OVERNIGHT EXCURSIONS

HIGHLIGHTS

- Gallipoli, see page 79
- Troy, see page 81

There are places of special interest that can be visited from Istanbul, but are sufficiently distant to require at least one overnight stop. They include the historic cities of Edirne, Bursa and İznik, and in winter there's a ski resort at Mount Uludağ, south of Bursa. Troy and Gallipoli are also very popular, and visiting them usually involves an overnight stay in **Çanakkale**, a seaside resort with hotels, restaurants and amenities, which also has a good Archaeological Museum.

GALLIPOLI

The **Gallipoli Peninsula** ㉗ *(Gelibolu Yarımadası)*, on the north side of the Dardanelles, was the scene of one of the most notorious military campaigns of World War I. The Allied assault, involving Australian, British, New Zealand and French forces, aimed to capture the peninsula and control the narrow strait of the Dardanelles, thus securing an ice-free sea passage to supply arms to Russia and open a front against the Germans.

The first landings took place on 25 April 1915, and met with fierce resistance from the Turks, under the command of General Mustafa

Arnavutköy mansions

Kemal. The Allies only managed to gain a toehold on the peninsula, and then deadlock ensued, with almost nine months of static trench warfare. The cost in human lives was severe, with 160,000 Allies and 86,000 Turks killed and some 250,000 wounded. The Anzacs (Australia and New Zealand Army Corps) saw some of the worst fighting and suffered the heaviest casualties; the beach where they landed has been named **Anzac Cove** *(Anzak Köyü)* in their honour.

The whole peninsula is a memorial, with plaques describing the campaign's progress, and monuments to the soldiers of the Allied and Turkish armies. Start either at the New Zealand Memorial at Chunuk Bair to take in the sweeping view of the battlefield or at the monumental **Çanakkale Epic Presentation Centre** in Kabatepe (Çanakkale Destanı Tanıtım Merkezi; charge), opened in 2012, to

Feyton driver on Büyükada, largest of the Princes' Islands

THE TROJAN HORSE

Most people know the story of the Trojan War as Homer told it. It all started when peace-loving King Priam's son, Paris, was inveigled by a trio of jealous goddesses into abducting the most beautiful woman in the world, Helen, wife of Menelaus, king of Sparta.

The ensuing war between Greece and Troy lasted 10 years and cost the lives of great heroes such as Hector and Achilles. The end came when the Greeks tricked the Trojans into accepting a gift of a huge wooden horse within their walls – it was filled with armed men who sacked the city and left it in ruins.

watch a multimedia presentation of the battle. Each war cemetery is signposted, and all are beautifully tended, planted with flowers and scented with fragrant hedges of rosemary. A memorial service attended by families of Turkish and Anzac veterans as well as other visitors is held each year on Anzac Day (25 April).

TROY

The exact location of the legendary city of **Troy** (https://muze.gov.tr; charge) remained a mystery until an amateur archaeologist with a passion for Homer began excavations in 1871. Heinrich Schliemann found his fabled city, and discovered 'Priam's treasure', a cache of gold. He smuggled it back to Germany, but it vanished during World War II, only to make a dramatic reappearance in Moscow in 1993.

Archaeologists have now uncovered nine superimposed cities, from Troy I, an Early Bronze Age settlement (3000–2500BC) to the Hellenistic and Roman metropolis, known as Ilium Novum, which stood here from 334BC to AD400. American scholars identify the level known as Troy VIIa as King Priam's city, and place its destruction around 1260BC. Certain eminent Turkish archaeologists disagree, instead opting for the preceding level, Troy VI.

The site, near the village of **Hısarlık**, is marked by a large replica of the famed wooden horse. For those who have enjoyed

The Aegean coastline

Homer's *Iliad* and *Odyssey* it is a magical place, where the stones are haunted by the spirits of Helen and Paris, Achilles and Agamemnon.

AEGEAN COAST

HIGHLIGHTS

- İzmir and the Northern Aegean, see page 83
- Pergamon, see page 86
- Sardis, see page 87
- Çeşme, see page 89
- Kuşadası and Environs, see page 90
- Efes (Ephesus), see page 91
- Pamukkale and Hierapolis, see page 94

» South of Kuşadası, see page 95
» Bodrum, see page 96

Turkey's Aegean coast offers an unparalleled combination of natural beauty and historical interest. This was one of the most densely populated parts of the ancient world, with many famous cities to its name – Troy, city of the *Iliad* and the *Odyssey*, and Smyrna (İzmir), the birthplace of Homer; Sardis, home of the wealthy King Croesus; Ephesus, where St Paul preached the gospels; and Halicarnassos, birthplace of the historian Herodotus. The ruins of two of the Seven Wonders of the World – the Temple of Artemis at Ephesus and the Mausoleum of Halicarnassus – are also to be found here.

Set amid these historic sites are many beautiful beaches and pretty fishing villages, and a number of modern holiday resorts, notably Kuşadası and Bodrum. The main city is İzmir, which has an international airport; there are other airports at Bodrum and Dalaman, where most package tours arrive.

İZMIR AND THE NORTHERN AEGEAN

Known to the Greeks as Smyrna, and to the Turks as *Güzel İzmir* (Beautiful İzmir), Turkey's third-largest city sprawls around the head of the finest natural harbour on the Aegean coast. **İzmir** 28 was founded in the 3rd millennium BC on the north shore of the bay, and reached a peak during the 10th century BC, when it was one

NOTES

The Aegean is named after King Aegeus, whose adopted son, Theseus, went off to kill the Minotaur, helped by Ariadne, who loved him. He deserted her, and so taken up was he with his adventures, he forgot a promise to change the black mourning sail from his ship for a white one. As his ship sailed home, Aegeus, seeing the black sail, thought Theseus was dead and threw himself to his death in the water.

of the most important cities in the Ionian Federation – the poet Homer was born in Smyrna during this period. After the Lydian conquest in the 6th century BC the city lost its importance, but was refounded by Alexander the Great on the slopes of Mount Pagus (now Kadifekale). Under the Greeks and Romans it became one of the principal centres of Mediterranean trade.

When the Ottoman Turks took control in the 15th century, İzmir grew wealthy as a merchant city, handling Smyrna figs and Turkish tobacco from the farms of the interior, and allowing the establishment of European trading colonies. It prospered as a port until the close of the Greco–Turkish War in 1922, when it was almost completely destroyed by bitter fighting and fire. Rebuilt around the site of Alexander's city, it is once again a bustling port and industrial city,

Konak Meydanı

> **NOTES**
>
> İzmir has a sizeable black community, the Turkish-speaking descendants of slaves from the Sudan, who were brought to Turkey in the 16th to 19th centuries.

the third largest in Turkey, but almost no trace remains of its former glory.

The heart of the city is **Konak Meydanı**, a square distinguished by two famous monuments. The **Clock Tower** *(Saat Kulesi)*, dating from 1901, is the unofficial symbol of İzmir. Nearby stands the tiny **Konak Camii** (mosque), built in 1756 and decorated with colourful Kütahya tile panels. On the hill to the south of the square stands the **Archaeological Museum** (https://izmir.ktb.gov.tr/EN-240789/izmir-archeology-museum.html, charge), whose superb collection of antiquities includes statues of Poseidon and Demeter that once stood in the Agora of ancient Smyrna. The nearby **Ethnographic Museum** (*Etnografya Muzesi*; https://izmir.ktb.gov.tr/EN-240791/izmir-ethnography-museum.html; charge) recreates such treats as the interiors of traditional local houses, an Ottoman pharmacy, a bridal chamber, a circumcision room, and exhibits on the manufacture of the 'evil eye' amulets and camel wrestling. Inland from the Konak Mosque is İzmir's **bazaar**, one of the best in Turkey.

North of Konak Meydanı, **Atatürk Caddesi** (also known as the **Kordon**) runs along the waterfront to the ferry port at Alsancak, 3km (2 miles) away. A horse-drawn *fayton* will take you on a tour, which passes through **Cumhuriyet Meydanı** (Republic Square), the centre of modern İzmir, surrounded by glittering luxury hotels and palm-fringed promenades. Nearby is the **Kültür Parkı**, a huge, shady pleasure garden, venue of the annual İzmir International Fair. Uphill, through the huge bazaar, lies the **Agora** (daily 8am–5pm; summer 9am–7pm), one of the few remaining traces of İzmir's ancient history. This colonnaded square, built during the 2nd century AD, was once the city's bustling marketplace. At the top of the

Trajaneum at Pergamon

hill is the imposing medieval fortress of **Kadifekale**. This was the ancient Mount Pagus, where Alexander the Great commanded his generals Lysimachus and Antigonus to found a new city in the 4th century BC. However, no trace remains of their original fortifications.

PERGAMON

The modern city of Bergama is 171km (107 miles) north of İzmir, towered over by the ruins of **Pergamon** ㉙. The **Bergama Archaeological Museum** (www.ktb.gov.tr; charge) is in the centre of the modern town, housing a large collection of material from Stone Age to Byzantine times.

At the height of its power, in the 2nd century BC, Pergamon (daily 8am–5pm, summer until 7pm) was one of the most splendid cities on the Aegean coast. Its acropolis was capped with magnificent buildings, and it had a library of over 200,000 volumes (the Pergamenes are credited with the invention of parchment). Its ruins, high above the modern town of Bergama, are still impressive.

The **acropolis** was built on a set of terraces. On the left of the entrance ramp is the open space once occupied by the **Temple of Athena**, close to which are the remains of the **Pergamene Library**. Its contents were eventually given to the beautiful Cleopatra as a gift from Mark Antony, and went to enrich the famous library of Alexandria.

Beyond the library is **Trajaneum**, the city's most splendid building, its glittering white marble columns, now partly restored. It was erected during the 2nd century AD in honour of the deified emperors Trajan and Hadrian.

Below the Temple of Athena is the steep *cavea* of the **theatre**, set in a shallow depression in the hillside. Nearby is the base of the **Altar of Zeus**, built to commemorate the defeat of the Gauls by the Romans in 190BC. This was once decorated with a remarkable frieze depicting the Battle of the Gods and Giants, one of the finest existing examples of Hellenistic sculpture, which now resides in Berlin's Pergamon Museum.

Visible on the plain below is the **Asclepion**, one of the ancient world's leading medical centres, rivalling similar establishments at Epidauros, Kos and Ephesus. Dedicated to Asclepius, god of healing, the Asclepion provided hot baths, massages, dream interpretation, primitive psychiatry, and draughts of water from a sacred spring (found to be mildly radioactive). Galen (AD130–200), the most famous physician in the ancient world after Hippocrates, practised here.

The entrance to the Asclepion is along a colonnaded street, the Sacred Way, which leads to the **medical precinct**. Here you can see the remains of the library, the theatre and the treatment rooms. In the middle of the square is a pool fed by the sacred spring.

SARDIS

The site of **Sardis** (http://sardisexpedition.org; charge) is usually visited from İzmir, though the nearest accommodation is Salihili which is just 9km (6 miles) away. Sardis, the former capital of ancient Lydia, is 100km (60 miles) east of İzmir, on the road to Uşak and Afyon.

Sardis was once the wealthiest city in the world, under the famous King Croesus (reigned 560–546BC), hence the expression 'rich as Croesus'. During his reign, the Lydians invented coinage,

Sardis Gymnasium

producing the first-ever coins of gold and silver, stamped with the royal emblem: a lion's head. The gold was washed down from the hills by the River Pactolus; the Greek historian Herodotus relates how flakes of the precious metal were trapped in the fleece of sheepskins spread in the stream-bed, perhaps giving rise to the legend of the Golden Fleece.

Intent on expanding his empire into Persian-held territory, Croesus consulted the oracle at Delphi. It told him that if he attacked the Persians he would destroy a great empire. He attacked anyway, and was crushed – the empire he destroyed was his own. The monuments you see today date from Roman and Byzantine times.

The principal ruins of Sardis are in two parts. On the left side of the main highway you will find the **Gymnasium complex**. From the car park you follow a line of **ancient shops** to a gate at the far end, which leads into the **synagogue**, whose floor is richly decorated with mosaic patterns. The gymnasium itself, a huge open square, is dominated by the magnificently restored **Marble Court**, lined with ornate marble columns and niches that once held statues. The arched gateway leads to a large swimming pool and the ruins of a Roman and Byzantine **baths** complex.

In the nearby village, a road leads south for 1km (0.75 mile) to the imposing **Temple of Artemis** (separate charge) begun during the reign of Alexander the Great, and abandoned, unfinished, following the ascendancy of Christianity in the 4th century. The enormous structure had a peristyle of 52 columns, of which two still stand at their full height. A 5th-century Byzantine church hides behind the columns at the far end.

ÇEŞME

A six-lane toll motorway leads 80km (50 miles) west of İzmir to the small resort and ferry port of Çeşme, where boats cross daily to the Greek island of Chios, a mere 12km (7.5 miles) away. The town was a quiet spa and beach resort (its name means 'drinking fountain') until the motorway's arrival brought it within comfortable

MARY'S HOUSE

Legend has it that St John the Apostle brought the Virgin Mary to Ephesus around AD37–48. Situated in the Bulbul Hills just south of Ephesus, the Meryemana (Mary's House) is where she is thought to have passed the last years of her life. It was discovered during the 19th century by priests from İzmir following instructions given by a German nun, Anna Katharina Emmerich, who had seen it in a vision. There is now a chapel occupying the site, which has long been a place of pilgrimage, but the building's foundations may date from the 1st century. Whether you're religious or not, it's a lovely walk into the pine-scented hills.

commuting distance of the city; now it is set to become a bustling seaside suburb of İzmir, and a terminal for international ferries from Italy and Greece.

The town is dominated by an Ottoman **fortress** (charge), built in the 16th century. Beside the fortress lies a 16th-century **caravanserai**, or inn, which has been converted into a luxury boutique hotel. On the main shopping street, among the many carpet and jewellery shops, you will find an attractive and interesting art gallery housed in the ancient Greek basilica of Ayios Haralambos.

There are a few other sights to see – the main attractions are the golden-sand **beaches at Ilıca**, home to several **hot springs**. The warm, sulphurous waters (around 35–50°C/95–122°F) are said to be good for rheumatism and respiratory complaints.

KUŞADASI AND ENVIRONS

Situated on a small promontory, **Kuşadası**, meaning 'Island of Birds', is one of Turkey's liveliest and most popular holiday resorts. The town, 80km (50 miles) south of İzmir, has a large yachting marina, and serves as a port for Mediterranean cruise ships. Attractions here include some pleasant beaches, a vibrant nightlife mainly geared to British and Irish holidaymakers, and the nearby ruins of Ephesus.

Whitewashed houses climb the hill above the harbour, where ferries depart daily for the Greek island of Samos, and lively bars and restaurants line the streets of the old quarter. The busy **bazaar** clusters around the walls of a 17th-century *caravanserai*, now converted into a hotel; across the street, seafood restaurants skirt the quay of the old harbour.

Beyond the modern ferry port, a 350m (1,050ft) causeway connects Kuşadası to **Güvercin Adası** (Pigeon Island), which is topped by a 13th-century Byzantine castle and ringed with gardens and colourful cafés.

A *dolmuş* (minibus) service links the town to the busy Ladies' Beach *(Kadınlar Plajı)*, 3km (2 miles) to the south, and there are also beaches at **Pamucak** and more peaceful ones in the **Dilek National Park** *(Dilek Yarımadası Milli Parkı*; charge), 25km (15.5 miles) from town.

EFES (EPHESUS)

Ephesus ㉚ is 17km (10.5 miles) inland from Kuşadası, and is usually visited on a trip from there, although the closest town is **Selçuk**, a small place 19km (12 miles) northeast of Kuşadası. Selçuk has taxis, restaurants, hotels and some lively bars, and the **Ephesus Museum** (https://muze.gov.tr; charge) has an exceptional archaeological section, including the famous 'many breasted Artemis';

Kuşadası, a lively and popular resort

and a fine ethnographical section. There are also several noteworthy monuments in and around town, including the 6th-century **Basilica of St John**, on Ayasuluk Hill, which supposedly marks the site of the Apostle's tomb. Above it is a fortress dating back to Byzantine times. Downhill you will find the impressive **Isa Bey Mosque** (1375), and beyond is a solitary column marking the site of the once-great **Temple of Artemis**.

Ephesus itself is one of the best-preserved and most visited of Turkey's ancient cities (https://visitephesus.org/en; charge). Its marble streets and monuments have been extensively excavated and restored, and it is easy to transport yourself back to Roman times.

Ionian Greeks from the island of Samos settled in Ephesus around 1000BC. The site was associated with the worship of the Anatolian mother-goddess Cybele, who became merged with the Greek Artemis. The great Temple of Artemis, one of the Seven Wonders of the World, was erected in her honour. The city was ruled in turn by the Lydians, the Persians and the Attalid kings of Pergamon, until 133BC, when Attalus III bequeathed his kingdom, and Ephesus with it, to the Romans. Ephesus was one of the most important cities in the new province of Asia, with a population of 200,000, and grew wealthy on the proceeds of trade. But its greatness was linked to its fine harbour, and when this silted up in the 3rd century AD, the city went into decline. The site was rediscovered by the British archaeologist J.T. Wood in 1869. Many of the ruins you see today date from the Roman period, between the 1st century BC and the 2nd century AD.

Most guided tours begin at the **Magnesian Gate** and head downhill along the main street. The first buildings inside the gate are the well-preserved **Odeum** (council chamber), with its semicircular seats, and the **Prytaneum**, where archaeologists found the two statues of Artemis, now on display in the Selçuk Museum. The marble-paved **Street of the Curetes**, its stone rutted by ancient cart wheels, leads through the Gate of Hercules to the remarkable **Temple of Hadrian**, with an arched doorway capped by the head of Tyche, the goddess of fortune. At the corner of Marble Street, on the right, are the **Baths of Scholastica**, which also included a brothel.

Rising up ahead is the imposing facade of the **Library of Celsus**, built in AD110 by a Roman consul as a memorial to his father. Beautiful statues of the four virtues – Episteme (Knowledge), Sophia (Wisdom), Ennoia (Thought) and Arete (Valour) – adorn the niches between the columns.

Marble Street leads from the library to the **Great Theatre**, the probable setting for the riot of the silversmiths described in the Bible (Acts 19:24–41). Its vast *cavea* provided seating for 25,000

Ephesus Amphitheatre

Petrified waterfalls at Pamukkale

people, and still accommodates the crowds who gather for performances during the annual International Festival of Arts and Culture (see page 110). From the top rows of seats you can enjoy a grand view of the Arcadian Way, the city's colonnaded main street, once lined with fine statues, and lit by oil lamps at night.

Pamukkale and Hierapolis

One popular excursion from the Aegean resorts is to the spectacular travertine terraces of **Pamukkale** ㉛ (Cotton Castle; daily sunrise–sunset), above the town of **Denizli**, about 200km (125 miles) inland from Kuşadası.

This remarkable natural formation has been created by mineral-rich hot springs cascading down the hillside and depositing layers of calcium carbonate. The resulting pools, terraces and 'petrified waterfalls' of dazzling white travertine are one of Turkey's most famous sights. The ruins of ancient **Hierapolis** lie scattered on the hillside behind the terraces, adding historical interest to natural beauty. The **Antique Pool** is a therapeutic, restorative spring whose waters will float you above a picturesque jumble of broken columns and Corinthian capitals.

A trip to Pamukkale also usually includes a visit to the site of the ancient city of **Aphrodisias** (https://aphrodisias-excavations.com; charge). The city, dedicated to the worship of Aphrodite, goddess of love, was famous for its superb sculpture. The ruins, which are still being excavated, include one of the best-preserved stadia in Turkey, 228m (748ft) long, with seating for 30,000, and the remarkable Sebasteion, a porticoed gallery of sculpture dedicated to Aphrodite and the Roman Emperor.

The hotels are all in the village of Karahayıt, on the plateau nearby, which has multi-coloured travertines, hot springs and spas and excellent, ridiculously cheap cotton clothing.

SOUTH OF KUŞADASI

Between Selçuk and Bodrum lie three important archaeological sites that can all easily be seen in one day.

Priene (8.30am–sunset), once one of the most active ports in the Ionian Federation, now stands about 5km (3 miles) inland, due to the silting up of the River Maeander. It enjoys a beautiful location on a higher terrace overlooking the plain, backed by the steep crag of the acropolis. The theatre, *bouleterion* (council chamber) and agora are worth exploring, but the main attraction is the great **Temple of Athena**. Alexander the Great, who passed through the city in 334BC, paid for its completion; five of the original 30 columns have been restored to their full height.

The silt of the River Maeander has also stranded the once-mighty city of **Miletus** (charge). Its harbour, from which Milesian ships set forth to found more than 100 colonies during the 7th and

8th centuries BC, is now a frog-filled marsh. Some idea of its former glory can be gleaned from the ruins of the agora, theatre and the Baths of Faustina.

No city ever stood at **Didyma**, just the colossal **Temple of Apollo**, one of the largest and most elegant temples in the ancient world. Only two columns still stand, but the forest of massive marble stumps gives some idea of the grandeur of the original building. People would travel great distances to consult the oracle of Apollo, seeking advice on business issues, marriage and military campaigns. When the Persians destroyed Miletus in 494BC, they also razed the Temple of Apollo at Didyma. Its reconstruction was begun by Alexander the Great (his victory over the Persians at Gaugamela in 331BC was predicted by the oracle), and continued for centuries, but the temple was never completed – some of the columns remain unfluted.

BODRUM

The picture-postcard resort of **Bodrum**, dubbed the St Tropez of Turkey, occupies the site of ancient Halicarnassos, famed as the city of King Mausolus, whose tomb was one of the Seven Wonders of the World, as well as the birthplace of Herodotus, the 'Father of History'. Little remains of Halicarnassos, however, and the town's main attractions include its laid-back, Bohemian atmosphere, a beautiful double bay backed by whitewashed houses, and the magnificent **Crusader Castle** that dominates the harbour. The attractions of

NOTES

There are no good beaches in Bodrum itself, but you have the choice of taking a boat trip from the harbour to one of the many coves that line the peninsula to the west. Most of the hotels that claim to be in Bodrum are actually in one of the many heavily developed villages on this peninsula, including Turgutreis, Gümüşlük, Yalıkavak and Türkbükü.

Bodrum, however, have not gone unnoticed – it gets very crowded during the summer.

The **Castle of St Peter** (www.bodrum-museum.com; charge) was built in the 15th century by the Knights of St John, who used stone quarried from the ruins of the Mausoleum of Halicarnassos. It fell to the Ottomans in 1523, and its various buildings now house a fine collection of antiquities, including a fascinating **Museum of Underwater Archaeology**. Among the highlights are the medieval Glass Wreck, the Kas-Uluburun Shipwreck, the Late Roman Shipwreck and the Hall of the Carian Princess with a royal tomb from about 360BC. The **towers** offer splendid views across the town and harbour. In the **English Tower**, the banqueting hall has been restored, and you can read the graffiti carved in the window niches by homesick knights.

Castle of St Peter, Bodrum

The site of the **Mausoleum** (same hours and website as Castle), the tomb of King Mausolus, is set a few blocks in from the harbour. It was begun around 355BC at the behest of the king (the word 'mausoleum' is derived from his name) and remained standing until at least the 12th century. By the time the Crusaders arrived in 1402 it was in ruins, destroyed by an earthquake. Today, nothing remains except the foundations. An exhibition hall displays several versions of how the building may have looked.

Pencil boxes made of bone on sale at the Grand Bazaar

Things to do

CULTURE

CLASSICAL ARTS

The re-opening of the Atatürk Cultural Centre (https://akmistanbul.gov.tr) in 2021 has breathed new life into Istanbul's classical arts scene, with a full roster of music, dance, and theatre performances. The Kadiköy Süreyya Opera House (https://sureyyaoperasi.kadikoy.bel.tr) is another leading venue.

Although technically outlawed by Atatürk's secularisation laws, the whirling dervishes (a Sufi mystical order) survive as a cultural heritage attraction, and give regular *sema* (whirling) performances at the Galata Mevlevi House (https://muze.gen.tr/muze-detay/galatamevlevi).

You'll likely hear traditional *fasil* (Ottoman court) music in bars and restaurants, especially the restaurants in Nevezade Sokak where wandering musicians play for diners. The side streets off İstiklal Caddesi, near the Taksim end, often have live shows in the local bars; check the boards outside for listings.

POPULAR MUSIC

Turkey has developed its own exuberant pop scene, with influences coming from folk rhythms, traditional tunes, the tango (which was at one time popular) and Arab and Western pop music. Timeless, well-known Turkish pop stars are Mustafa Sandal, Nilufer and Sezen Aksu. Singer-songwriter Tarkan has achieved superstar status – although it's rare to see these international performers in concert within Turkey.

The Istanbul International Music Festival (www.iksv.org), held from mid-June to mid-July, hosts musicians and performers from all over the world in various venues. Jazz is popular in Istanbul, and many bars and clubs have live bands performing at weekends; some specialist venues have jazz nightly.

TURKISH BATHS

No trip to Turkey would be complete without a visit to the *hamam*, or Turkish bath. There are three historic baths in Istanbul that cater specifically for tourists, namely the 16th-century Cemberlitas Hamamı (www.cemberlitashamami.com), the 18th-century Çağaloğlu Hamamı (www.cagalogluhamami.com.tr) (both in Sultanahmet), and the 16th-century Tarihi Galatasaray Hamamı (www.galatasarayhamami.com) in Beyoğlu. These places are worth a visit for their interior marble architecture alone, but the opportunity to experience a genuine Turkish bath should not be missed. There are usually separate entrances for men (*erkek*) and women (*kadın*), but if there is only one chamber, then different times are set aside for men and women. Most are open from at least 8am to 8pm; longer hours for men.

Carpets at the Grand Bazaar

Leave your valuables in a locker at the desk and get undressed in the changing room. Wearing a towel and bath clogs, you will be shown to the steamy marble washroom, where buckets of hot water will be poured over you before an attendant sets to work with a coarse glove, removing dirt and dead skin and leaving you pink and glowing. You can also have a massage at this point (for an additional charge). Afterwards, you retire to the changing room for tea or a drink, feeling completely relaxed and rejuvenated.

You can also try out mud and spa treatments, and massages, which are considered beneficial for many medical conditions.

SHOPPING

Istanbul's markets and bazaars offer some of the world's most interesting – and challenging – opportunities for shopping. A huge variety of handmade goods finds its way into the city from towns and villages all over Turkey, much of it of very high quality – wool and silk carpets, kilims (flat-weave rugs), *cicims* (embroidered kilims), leather goods, ceramics and pottery, copper and brassware, and jewellery.

The principal shopping area in Istanbul is the Grand Bazaar, with more than 4,000 shops crammed beneath its roof. Running downhill from here is Uzunçarşı Caddesi, lined with hardware shops, which leads to the Spice Bazaar, the best place to buy *lokum* (Turkish Delight). Across from Beyazit square are the backstreets of Laleli, the place to look for low-priced clothes, especially leather jackets. Shopping isn't confined to the market. For more modern up-market shopping, try the stylish boutiques of Nişantaşı and Teşvikiye, near Taksim Square, or head west for international designer brands to the Galleria shopping mall by the marina at Ataköy or east to the Kanyon Mall in Levent. There are also plenty of smart shops along İstiklal Caddesi. For craft shops, antique dealers and bijou galleries, try Çukurcuma in Galatasaray, or Ortaköy on a Saturday or Sunday. For leather go to Zeytinbürnu, halfway to the airport.

BARGAINING

Unless you're in a fixed-price shop, bargaining for handicrafts and souvenirs is a way of life, especially in the Grand Bazaar. If you are buying more than one of anything, try and bring the price down even more. Shop around (especially if it's a major purchase) and find out how much shopkeepers ask, then offer about half what you are prepared to pay. (Fixed-price shops, especially for carpets, are a good way to gauge prices.) The owner will feign amazement at your insultingly low offer, you will plead poverty, and add that you can get it cheaper elsewhere. Good-natured banter continues until you reach a mutually acceptable price. Large purchases can take several glasses of tea and a good half-hour's discussion. Never begin bargaining for something you don't intend to buy, and never quote a price you are not prepared to pay. Traders are often aware that tourists are uncomfortable bargaining, so they simply offer a 'best price'. This is the least they'll be able to accept and there's no point discussing it as their profit margins are slender. Items on sale in the resorts are not always of the best quality.

WHAT TO BUY

You need an export licence to take a genuine antique out of the country, and this involves getting a certificate. If you buy an old-looking item, even if it's clearly fake, get a *fatura*, an invoice, from the dealer stating the piece's value and when and where it was made, because the customs people may need convincing. A reputable dealer will organise a certificate for you.

Carpets and kilims. No two carpets are identical. Patterns and symbols have significance, conferring good luck and protection from the evil eye. Carpets and kilims from different regions of Turkey differ in design and colours, and even more so when they are from overseas, as is increasingly the case.

Carpet prices reflect the age, rarity, quality of materials and dyes, and tightness of weave. The number of knots in a square centimetre ranges from 20–30 for a coarse wool carpet to 100–200 in a silk carpet. The amount of work is reflected in the price. Natural dyes cost more than synthetic ones. It is worth doing your homework, and asking a few pertinent questions will make the seller less likely to fob you off with an inferior item. Kilims are rugs that are woven, rather than knotted. A *cicim* is a kilim with embroidered decoration.

Ceramics and pottery. The kilns at İznik near Bursa produced the best ceramic tiles ever, and these are now collector's items. You'll have to make do with polychrome tiles, bowls and vases, some of which copy the traditional designs but are affordable.

Copper and brassware

Copper and brass. Hand-beaten pieces are available in the shops of the Old Bedesten in the Grand Bazaar and on Bakircilar Caddesi, behind Beyazıt Square, where braziers, shoeshine boxes, lamps, candlesticks, coffee grinders and samovars are ready to buy. Coppersmiths may even make items to order or engrave a purchase.

Leather and suede. Handbags, wallets, belts, jackets, trousers, coats and skirts are all bargains. The leather is generally good quality but sometimes the stitching is poor, so check on the workmanship before you commit yourself. Clothing and shoes can be made to order, but good-quality work takes time.

Jewellery. The best place to look for quality jewellery is Old Bedesten in the Grand Bazaar. Some cheaper items can be found in Kalpakcilar Basi Caddesi (the main street of the bazaar). Gold is sold by weight, and prices are posted daily. There's a surcharge for workmanship. Genuine sterling silver is hallmarked. Beware of cheap imitations with fake stones and silver plating, especially in

> **NOTES**
>
> For English books about Turkish culture and history, try Homer Kitabevi, 12A Yenicarsi Caddesi, Galatasaray (www.homerbooks.com); Robinson Crusoe 389, 195A Istiklal Caddesi (www.rob389.com); Galeri Kayseri, Divanyolu 58, Sultanahmet (www.galerikayseri.com) and Minoa Books & Coffe, Vişnezade, 52A Süleyman Seba Cd. (https://minoa.com).

shops in resorts. For contemporary local designer jewellery, browse the tiny shops in Çukurcuma, or in Nişantaşi.

Clothing. Turkey is one of the world's largest suppliers of cotton and cotton clothing, including many big-name brands. Good-quality cotton clothing is excellent value, while the resorts often have great designer boutiques. You can pick up great bargains of 'slight seconds' of designer gear at rock-bottom prices in Iş Merkezi on İstiklal Caddesi.

Other items. In the resorts sponges of all shapes and sizes can be found. A speciality of Bodrum is hand-crafted leather sandals. You might consider buying a sheesha pipe, a nargile, the kind smoked by old men and trendy students in Turkish cafés, or a highly decorated chess or backgammon board. There are beautiful meerschaum pipes and figurines, too.

You can't leave without a *nazar boncuk*, the evil-eye amulet. If ever you find it cracked, it's done its job and you need a replacement. Prayer beads, traditional musical instruments and puppets also make good souvenirs.

ENTERTAINMENT

NIGHTLIFE

In Istanbul, nightlife is to be found on İstiklal Caddesi and the surrounding streets, around the Taksim and Beyoğlu area and along the European shore of the Bosphorus, especially at Ortaköy. There isn't much revelry in the old city, so if you prefer a quiet supper and early bed, that's the place for you. Of course, there are rip-off joints, where you will be charged an astronomical amount and forcibly relieved of your wallet if you don't pay up, but these are outnumbered by places which are good value. (Men travelling alone should resist the temptation to join a 'new friend' at his favourite bar or club; reports of pricey scams are still around.)

Istanbul has a thriving bar and club scene, with venues to suit every taste with DJs, live bands, dance music and rooftop cocktail bars. Aside from Turkish contemporary music, everything from jazz and rock to house and hip-hop is on offer, in some club or other. Turkey is somewhat ambivalent about gay life, but there are gay clubs and bars.

The Book Market (Sahasar Çarsısı) by the Grand Bazaar

Nightlife is a feature of the Aegean resorts – bars pump out music, live or otherwise, with Turkish or English lyrics. There is probably something for everyone among the ubiquitous English and Irish pubs and other bars, and the live entertainment. Turkish evenings and other treats are available.

CLUBS AND BARS

Although Islamic, Turkey is far from 'dry' and Istanbul's nightlife is some of the best and most varied in Europe. Most of it centres around Beyoğlu. In stylish rooftop bars like **360 Istanbul** (8/F Misir Apt, 163 İstiklal Caddesi; www.360istanbul.com) and **5. Kat** (3 Soganci Sokak, Cihangir; www.5kat.com) you can sip cocktails with the beautiful people while gazing at the city's panorama and the Bosphorus. Alternatively, join local bohemians drinking cold beer at **Arsen Lüpen**'s terrace (Mis Sokak No:15/4) with its superb views; or enjoy ingenious shots at trendy **Tektekçi** (Akarsu Sokak No.2/1) which is a perfect place to meet friends and start the evening.

Babylon (Şeybender Sokak, off Asmalimescit; http://babylon.com.tr) is one of Istanbul's best clubs for live bands from around the world, and top-class international DJs. If you prefer techno music and electronic sounds, try the popular **Temple** (Şehit Muhtar, 15 Mis Sk; www.facebook.com/ClubTemple).

BELLY DANCING

This ancient art is thought to have its origins in Africa. It is a popular entertainment for local people although mainly for tourists, and the best dancers are famous, often appearing on Turkish TV.

Most major dinner and belly-dancing shows are geared towards tourists, but inevitably some are lower quality than others, and some are just shameless rip-offs. To avoid falling for one of these, do your research and book ahead with a reputable show like Les Arts Turcs, a gallery and arts centre in Sultanahmet (Alemdar, 19 İncili Çavuş Sk; www.lesartsturcs.com).

If alfresco clubbing is your scene, you will like the summer-time outdoor clubs at Ortaköy, which attract local socialites and wannabes; phone to get on the guest list at **Sortie** (Kuruçeşme, 54 Muallim Naci Caddesi; https://sortie.com.tr) or **Ruby** (Yıldız, 5 Ortaköy Salhanesi; www.rubyistanbul.com).

A night out on Nevizade Street, off İstiklal

SPORTS

SPECTATOR SPORTS

Football is Turkey's favourite sport and there are three internationally famous Istanbul teams: Galatasaray, Fenerbahçe and Beşiktaş. Most years one of these teams wins the Turkish Superlig, although Trabzonspor surprised everyone by winning it in 2022. Check the local newspapers for home fixtures; Inönü Stadium, overlooking Dolmabahçe Palace, and home to Beşiktaş, is the most accessible and attractive venue.

The British media, in particular, has previously given much coverage to the perceived hostility of Turkish fans; however, trouble between fans is rare and the stadiums are heavily policed.

Unique to Turkey is the centuries-old national sport of oil wrestling *(yağlı güreş)*, with tournaments held in the summer. The largest and most famous is Kirkpinar, held in June near Edirne, 230km (143 miles) northwest of Istanbul. The competitors, wearing only

Oil wrestling is the national sport

a pair of leather breeches, coat themselves in olive oil and perform a ceremonial procession before getting to grips with their slippery opponents and flinging each other around, to the delighted cheers of thousands of spectators.

An even more exotic spectacle is camel wrestling *(deve güreşi)*, which takes place over the winter months (mating season) in small towns and villages around the Aegean cost. The biggest festival is held in January between Selçuk and Kuşadası. These one-humped beasts are bad-tempered, and when two moody males confront each other in the ring, a fierce sparring match ensues, in which they use their necks to try to throw each other off balance. The winning beast is the one that stays on its feet, and the match usually ends well before any injuries ensue.

Horse racing may seem rather tame by comparison. Races are held between April and December at the Veliefendi Hippodrome near Bakırköy, 15km (9 miles) west of Istanbul, organised by the Turkish Jockey Club (www.tjk.org). In winter, they move to İzmir.

Sadly, Turkey no longer hosts the Formula 1 Grand Prix at Tuzla.

ACTIVE PURSUITS

There are a couple of long-established golf courses. Klassis (http://klassis.org) is the best known. Alternatively, head for Kermer Golf

& Country Club situated about 25km (15.5 miles) northeast of the city-centre.

The polluted water around Istanbul means one needs to go to a beach outside the city. The best ones are within easy reach: the Black Sea resorts. There are good swimming beaches on the Princes' Islands, too, but they are extremely crowded at weekends. Kilyos, 35km (22 miles) west of the city, reached via minibus to Sariyer, has clean beaches (charge).

Water sports. The Aegean really comes into its own with water sports, including assorted forms of sailing, windsurfing, kitesurfing, scuba diving, snorkelling, paragliding, water skiing, canoeing, banana boat rides, jet skiing and more.

FESTIVALS AND EVENTS

January/February Camel-wrestling festival near Selçuk.

March Festival of Victory, Çanakkale. Celebrates the Turks' successful defence of the Dardanelles against British warships in World War I. Includes performances by the traditional Ottoman army mehter band.

April Istanbul International Film Festival organised by Istanbul Foundation for Culture and Arts (www.iksv.org), lasting for two weeks, featuring new releases of Turkish and foreign films. Anzac Day, Çanakkale (25 April), commemorates those killed in the Gallipoli campaign. International Istanbul Tulip Festival, best experienced at Emirgan Park with its several tulip gardens.

NOTES

Istanbul and the Bosphorus are special spots for migrating birds. Raptors are the main attraction, and most European species pass through, although some peak at different times. Keen birdwatchers should look out for honey and common buzzards, the lesser spotted eagle and the Levant sparrowhawk.

Banana boat ride at the coast

May Festival of Culture and Art at Selçuk and Ephesus, using the Great Theatre at Ephesus as a venue. Fatih Festivities, Istanbul, commemorating the conquest of Byzantium in 1453 by Sultan Fatih Mehmet (29 May).

June Istanbul International Music Festival (www.iksv.org), a world-class event featuring big names in opera and ballet at venues including Hagia Eirene. Associated with it is the Istanbul International Jazz Festival. Istanbul Pride Week culminates in the march for the LGBTQ+ community – at the time of writing this was officially banned, but events still took place most years regardless.

July Istanbul International Jazz Festival (www.iksv.org) takes place at various locations around the city. Istanbul Festivali (https://istanbulfestivali.com), multi-genre music festival in Festival Park Yenikapı. Oil wresting competition Kirkpinar near Edirne.

August Troy Festival, Canakkale. Five-day festival celebrating the discovery of ancient Troy with folk dance and sport competitions, concerts and street parades enacting the legend of Paris and Helen.

October–November International Arts Biennale, Istanbul (odd-numbered years), major visual arts event organised around an important political or philosophical theme (www.iksv.org). Marmaris International Yacht Race (www.miyc.org/en). Istanbul International Theatre Festival (www.iksv.org), even years only.

Food and drink

Turkey has one of the world's richest cuisines, with influences derived from the many cultures of the former Ottoman Empire, and top-quality produce from Anatolia's lush farmland and fertile seas. Many dishes originated in the kitchens of the Ottoman sultans; in the time of Süleyman the Magnificent there were more than 150 recipes for aubergines alone. Many eating places offer standard fare: soups, *meze*, salads, kebabs and seafood, but in Istanbul there's plenty of good international cuisine and top-quality hotel restaurants. From the 2010s onward, Istanbul's long-established street food scene expanded rapidly beyond *kebap* and *pide* stalls as taco trucks, coffee carts and seafood stands began to proliferate.

Fresh produce from markets

TOP 10 THINGS TO TRY

1. STARTERS (MEZE)

Meze is the collective name given to a wide selection of appetisers, both hot and cold. They are usually presented on a tray at your table, or in a glass-fronted display case, and you can choose as few or as many dishes as you like. The more popular offerings include *kuru fasulye* (haricot beans in tomato sauce), *patlıcan kizartması* (aubergine fried

Döner kebap

in olive oil and garlic), and *biber dolması* (green peppers stuffed with rice, raisins and pine nuts). *Meze* are served with fresh white bread, sometimes hot flat bread, to soak up the oil and juices.

2. SOUPS (ÇORBA)

Turkish soups are usually thick and substantial. Try *düğün çorbası* ('wedding' soup, a mutton broth flavoured with lemon juice and cayenne, and thickened with egg), *mercimek çorbası* (red-lentil soup), or *işkembe çorbası* (tripe soup, believed to be a hangover cure). *İşkembecis* stay open until the early hours of the morning to serve tripe soup to peckish late-night revellers on their way home.

3. KEBAP

Ask anyone to name a typically Turkish dish and the likely answer is *kebap* – grilled, broiled or roasted meat. The most common varieties include *şiş kebap* (cubes of lamb threaded on a skewer and grilled over charcoal) and *döner kebap* (literally 'revolving' kebab – a stack of marinated, sliced lamb and minced mutton roasted on a vertical spit, with slices cut off as the outer layers cook). The ubiquitous *İskender kebap* is a dish of *döner kebap* served on a bed of diced *pide* bread with tomato sauce and yoghurt, topped with a sizzling splash of browned butter.

4. KOFTE

Meatballs of minced lamb are called *köfte*. Almost as ubiquitous on Turkish menus as the various forms of *kebap*, they are variously served in rich sauces flavoured with tomato and aubergine, burger-style as grilled patties, deep-fried, with rice, and in myriad other ways.

5. STEW

Turkish cuisine's wide roster of hearty stews are particularly tempting on a chilly Istanbul winter's evening. One classic dish is *mantarlı güveç*, a delicious stew of tender lamb, mushrooms, peppers, tomatoes and garlic, all baked in a clay dish and topped with cheese.

6. SEAFOOD

The seas around Turkey abound with fish, and waterfront restaurants serve the catch of the day, sold by weight. Fish is usually twice the price of meat, so not a cheap option. Choose yours from the display and find out how much it will cost before having it cooked. The best way is simply grilled over charcoal. Some of the tastiest are *levrek* (sea bass), *barbunya* (red mullet), and *palamut* (bonito). Especially good is eating fish along the Bosphorus, whether in a pricey restaurant, or getting a cheap *balik ekmek* (fish sandwich) from a stall.

7. LOKUM

The best-known Turkish dessert is *lokum* (Turkish Delight), the most common variety being a soft jelly, flavoured with rosewater and sprinkled with icing sugar. One of many food and drink items whose origin is contested between

NOTES

Many confections have names that betray their origins in the harem –*dilber dudağı* (lips of the beloved), *hanım göbeği* (lady's navel) and *bülbül yuvası* (nightingale's nest).

Greeks and Turks, this is one for those with a serious sweet tooth.

Turkish tea

8. TEA

The Turkish national drink is *çay* (tea), drunk throughout the day, in shops, cafés and offices. Tea is usually served black and strong in small tulip-shaped glasses, with sugar lumps on the dinky saucer.

9. COFFEE

Turkish coffee *(kahve)* is strong, black and served complete with grounds in a small espresso cup, with a glass of water on the side. Sugar is added while brewing, so order *sade* (no sugar), *orta şekerli* or *çok şekerli* (very sweet). Leave it for a moment for the grounds to settle, and don't drain your cup. Most cafés serve cappuccino, latte and the like; for instant coffee, ask for Nescafé.

10. WINE

Turkish wines *(şarap)* have a history going back as far as 7000BC, and some believe that European vine-stocks may have originated here. Despite good quality local wines, Turks are not great wine drinkers although there is a growing appreciation. You can choose from a wide range of reds, whites, rosés and sparkling wines. You will always find Villa Doluca, Çankaya, Kavak and Dikmen; look out also for award-winning labels such as Kavaklidere and Likya.

Turkish-made beer is also good. Most popular is Efes Pilsen, which is produced in Istanbul and sold in almost every bar and restaurant in the country. Imported labels are also common.

WHERE TO EAT

Many of the eating places in Turkey specialise in serving a certain kind of dish. An average restaurant, offering a variety of typically Turkish food and drink, freshly prepared, is called a *restoran*, and may or may not be licensed. A *lokanta* is a simple canteen-type restaurant, for a quick filling feed rather than gastronomic delight, serving *hazır yemek* (ready food) where you choose from heated trays of pre-cooked food. In the *ocakbaşi* the barbecue grill cooks sizzling meats on skewers, and is a cosy eatery in winter months. A *gazino* is a restaurant serving alcohol, usually with an evening floor show of belly-dancing and folk music.

Turkish kahve

The range of informal, cheap eateries is vast. A *kebapçı* specialises in grilled meats, notably kebabs served with *pide* and salad, while a *pideci* or *pide salonu* is a Turkish-style pizza parlour, dishing up tasty *pide* (unleavened bread) topped with minced lamb, eggs or cheese. You can enjoy lamb meatballs in a *köfteci*, tripe in an *işkembeci*, soup in a *çorbacı*, and milk puddings in a *muhallebici*. A *büfe* is a street kiosk which sells

A büfe is a street kiosk selling snacks and soft drinks

snacks and soft drinks. See recommended restaurants, page 118.

ESSENTIAL INFORMATION

The typical Turkish breakfast, served between 7 and 10am, consists of bread, butter and jam, with olives, cucumber, tomato, white cheese and perhaps a hard-boiled egg, washed down with sweet black tea. *Menemen* is a delicious dish of eggs scrambled with tomatoes, green peppers and sometimes white cheese. People eat out regularly, and there are many restaurants, cafés and food stalls open all day and late into the evening. There are no set times for lunch and dinner, especially in tourist areas, and you can eat at almost any time of day.

A typical Turkish meal begins with a spread of *meze* (starters), washed down with *rakı*, followed by grilled meat, fish or kebabs, and rounded off with fresh fruit or *baklava*, and tiny cups of the famous strong black Turkish coffee. Don't order a main course until you have finished the *meze*; you may be too full to appreciate it. It is perfectly acceptable to have a meal composed entirely of *meze*.

Avoid drinking tap water, and stick to bottled mineral water, which is easily available everywhere – *maden suyu* is carbonated mineral water; *memba suyu* is still mineral water. A traditional Turkish thirst-quencher is *ayran*, a 50:50 mixture of yoghurt and mineral water, seasoned with a pinch of salt. Refreshing on its own, it's also often drunk with a meal especially in a *lokanta*. Freshly squeezed orange juice *(taze portakal sütu)* is available in season.

It's important to note that although alcohol is widely available, prices are high because of constantly increasing government taxes. The national alcoholic drink is a very potent anise liquor called *rakı*. It is drunk as an aperitif, and throughout a meal. It should be mixed half-and-half with iced water, with a glass of water on the side (when mixed with water it turns a pearly white, hence its nickname, *aslan sütü* – lion's milk). Beware of drinking it without food – it's stronger than you think and the after-effects are powerful.

MENU READER

Adana kebap – spicy minced beef moulded around a skewer and grilled
Aşure – sweet porridge made with cereals, nuts and fruit
Baklava –alternating layers of thin pastry and ground pistachios, almonds or walnuts, saturated with syrup
Bira – beer
Cacık – yoghurt with cucumber and garlic
Çiftlik kebap – a casserole of lamb, onion and peas
Fırın kebap – oven-roasted fillet of lamb marinated in yoghurt
Fırın sütlaç – baked rice pudding
Hamsi– whole fried anchovies
Kahve – coffee
Kılıç şiş – swordfish skewers
Lüfer – bluefish
Sigara böreğı – cheese-filled pastry rolls
Tarator – a cold yoghurt soup with dill, delicious in summer
Tavuk göğsü – a combination of rice, milk, sugar and chicken breast
Uskumru – mackerel
Vejetaryan – vegetarian
Zerde – a saffron-flavoured rice pudding

Places to eat

We have used the following symbols to give an idea of the price for a three-course meal for two, excluding drinks:

$ below £20
$$ £20–35
$$$ £35–60
$$$$ over £60

ISTANBUL

OLD CITY

Asitane Kariye Hotel, Kariye Camii Sokak 6, Edirnekapı, www.asitanerestaurant.com. Classic original Ottoman recipes and music in the setting of a peaceful garden neighbouring the Kariye Mosque. **$$$$**

Avlu Tevkifhane Sokak 1, Sultanhamet, www.fourseasons.com/istanbul. For a real splash-out meal, head for this rooftop restaurant at the Four Seasons Hotel, with magnificent views and world-class modern Anatolian cuisine. Reservations recommended. **$$$$**

Balikçi Sabahattin Cankurtaran Caddesi 1, Cankurtaran, www.balikcisabahattin.com. Top-quality seafood at this family-run restaurant, in a traditional Ottoman house in a quiet backstreet. Lovely terrace in summer. **$$$$**

Dubb Indian Restaurant Incili Cavus Sokak 10 (off Divan Yolu), Sultanahmet, www.dubbindian.com. Pleasant little spot with a roof terrace, serving decent Indian food, including tandoori lamb, chicken and vegetarian curries and hot naan breads. Good-value set meals. **$$$**

Hamdi Et Lokantasi Kalcin Sokak 11, Eminönü, www.hamdi.com.tr. Overlooking the Golden Horn, this huge, unpretentious venue specialises in grilled meat dishes; no alcohol. Reservations recommended for the terrace in summer. **$$$**

Havuzlu Gani Çelebi Sokak 3, Kapalı Çarşı, www.havuzlurestaurant.com. Traditional Turkish cuisine in the heart of the Grand Bazaar. Open for lunch only. Closed Sunday. **$$**

Mozaik Incirli Cavus Sokak 1, off Divan Yoly, Sultanahmet, tel: 0212-512 4177. Cosy, three-floored restaurant in a converted Ottoman house; this is on the tourist trail but a cut above the rest. The menu comprises Turkish dishes, such as *Abant* kebab (lamb with aubergine in terracotta pot), pasta and fillet steak. Good service. **$$–$$$**

Rami Utangaç Sokak 6, Sultanahmet, www.ramirestaurant.com. The impressionistic paintings of Turkish artist Rami Uluer are displayed in this romantic restaurant, set in a restored wooden mansion. Serving seafood and traditional Turkish dishes, you can watch the Blue Mosque's sound-and-light show from the terrace. **$$$$**

Tantunihan Mısır Çarşısı, Sultan Hamam Girişi, Yeni Cami Caddesi 47, Eminönü, www.babihayat.com. Beside the eastern entrance to the market, this popular restaurant specialises in *tantuni*, a popular fast-food dish of stir-fried lamb and vegetables, wrapped in *lavash* bread. Great for a shopping break. **$**

NEW CITY

Agatha Restaurant Mesrutiyet Caddesi 52, Tepebasi, http://perapalace.com. The fine dining venue in the Pera Palace Hotel is as stylish as you would expect, with top cuisine inspired by venues on the original fabled train route. **$$$$**

Any Bebek Caddesi No.71/A, Arnavutköy, www.facebook.com/anyistanbul. A trendy restobar serving international cuisine, in a neighbourhood full of fish and seafood restaurants. Popular at breakfast time and for evening cocktails. Live DJ shows make *Any* a perfect chill-out spot by the Boshporus. **$$$**

Canim Cigerim Minare Sokak, off Asmalimescit, Beyoğlu, tel: 0212-243 1005. Serving only skewered liver grilled over charcoal, with piles of salad and warm flatbread, this simple café lacks choice but makes up for in value. Always busy. No alcohol. **$**

Damo Katip Mustafa Çelebi, Hocazade Sk. 22, https://damorestaurant.com/en. This justifiably popular restaurant is well worth checking out for its fantastic Iranian cuisine. There are similarities with Turkish food – rice and spiced meats figure prominently – but there is more use of aromatics like almond and rosewater, and the uniquely Iranian dishes are highly distinctive. Try *ghormeh sabzi*, a stew of parsley, leeks and beans. **$$$**

Kafe Ara Tosbaga Sokak, off Yenicarsi Caddesi, tel: 0212-245 4105. High-ceilinged arty café owned by Istanbul's top photographer, Ara Güler, with his works lining the walls. Enjoy an informal meal of ravioli, steak or just have a coffee, inside or on the patio. Great for people watching. **$$–$$$**

Leb-i-Derya Kumbaraci Yokuşu 57/6, www.endamistanbul.com. One of three outlets in a small chain, with a tiny summer terrace, this trendy restaurant is one of *the* places to be seen. The international menu ranges from a full English breakfast to a 40-spiced steak to chocolate fondue – all heavenly. **$$$$**

Mikla The Marmara Pera, Mesrutiyet Caddesi 15, Beyoğlu, www.miklarestaurant.com. The top-floor restaurant, with a terrace, is one of Istanbul's most stylish, romantic venues, with Turkish-Scandinavian fusion from owner/chef Mehmet Gürs. Dinner only. **$$$$**

Nevizade Sokak Off Istiklal Caddesi, Beyoğlu. A narrow street filled with noisy *meyhanes* for *meze*, grilled meats and fish, as well as bars full of youngsters. Packed at weekends, a little quieter in the week, it makes for a fun and cosmopolitan night out. **$$$**

Suat Usta Mersin Tantuni Katip Mustafa Çelebi, Tel Sk. 1, https://suatustatantuni.com.tr. A simple venue specialising in *tantuni,* wraps, and meat sandwiches. **$$**

Suzy's Café du Levant Ramhi M.Koc Museum, Kumbarhane Caddesi 2, Sutluce, www.divan.com.tr. Gorgeous café in the grounds of Turkey's first industrial museum, serving French bistro food; wonderful views over the Golden Horn. **$$$$**

Vogue Spor Caddesi, BJK Plaza, A Block, Floor 13, Süleyman Seba Caddesi, Beşiktaş, https://voguerestaurantandbar.com. Über-chic restaurant with a fabulous range of sushi, plus a vast range of wines. Style is everything here. Gorgeous terrace in summer. Reservations essential. **$$$$**

BOSPHORUS

Banyan Muallim Naci Caddesi, Salhane Sokak 3, Ortaköy, www.banyan-restaurant.com. Authentic southeast Asian cuisine at this sunny seafront restaurant, with tasty satays, Thai green curries, and crunchy Vietnamese salads. **$$$**

Çiya Güneslibahçe Sokak 43, 44 and 48, Kadiköy, www.ciya.com.tr. Three separate sites for this amazingly popular, good-value kebab restaurant with imaginative dishes from all over Turkey; vegetarians also catered for. Try for an outdoor table on the street. No alcohol. **$$–$$$**

Kanaat Lokantasi Selmanipak cd. No:9 Üsküdar, www.kanaatlokantasi.com.tr. An institution and much admired, Kanaat was established in 1933 and is a family concern serving time-honoured recipes. Plenty of tables and always bustling, it's just a step away from the Üsküdar ferry terminal. No alcohol or credit cards. **$$**

Lacivert Körfez Caddesi 57A, Kanlıca, www.lacivertrestaurant.com. On the Asian side of the Bosphorus, near Sultan Mehmet Bridge, but with boat service from the European side, Lacivert is famed for its Sunday brunch. DJs provide music. **$$$**

Lucca Cevdetpasa Caddesi 51, Bebek, www.luccastyle.com. A self-styled 'Bistronomique' lounge and bar, this chic arty venue is very popular with trendy local people. Come here for Med-American cuisine, tapas and lemon sea bass. House DJs play after-dinner sounds. **$$$**

THE AEGEAN

BODRUM

The Marmara Tuti Marmara Bodrum, Suluhasan Caddesi 18, www.themarmarahotels.com. Top-class dining on the rooftop of this luxury boutique hotel, with stunning sea views. Varied menu includes jumbo shrimps stuffed with ginger, and linguine with bacon. **$$$$**

Trança Çarşı, Dr. Alim Bey Cd. 32, https://trancarestaurant.eatbu.com. Seaside fish restaurant with outdoor terrace. Simple menu, delicious food. Great views of sea and castle. **$$**

CANAKKALE

Yalova Gümrük Sokak 7, Liman Caddesi, https://yalovarestoran.com. The best of a number of fish restaurants lining the seafront in Çanakkale. Good views, a rooftop terrace and convenient location near the ferry port. Open all year. **$$$**

IZMIR

Deniz Atatürk Caddesi 188/B, Alsancak, www.denizrestaurant.com.tr. Commonly regarded as the best fish restaurant in town, with tables spilling onto the seafront pavement in summer. Open all year. **$$$**

KUŞADAŞI

Tarihi Cinar Balik Next to Kismet Otel, Akyar, tel: 0256-618 1847. This gorgeous fish restaurant seems far away from the buzz of the resort, and serves fresh fish in a simple setting. **$$$**

SELÇUK

Okumus Mercan Restaurant PTT Karsisi Hal Bina 43 (opp PTT), tel: 0232-892 6196. In the town centre; fresh fish and plenty of vegetarian dishes are served in this pretty leafy courtyard. **$$**

Travel essentials

PRACTICAL INFORMATION

ACCESSIBLE TRAVEL

Few major sights have elevators or ramps, and wheelchairs are not permitted inside mosques, but the new green buses have wheelchair facilities, as do most tram stations. Accessible public toilets are harder to come by. There's a support association called the Bedensel Engellilerle Dayanışma Denerği (www.bedd.org.tr).

ACCOMMODATION

Hotels in Turkey are classified from one to five stars and there is accommodation to suit everyone. If you want a lively place in Istanbul, go to Taksim-Beyoğlu where many international hotels are located as well as some good inexpensive options, luxury boutique hotel and apart-hotels. Peace and quiet is available in the Old City. Sultanahmet has plenty of reasonable establishments including restored Ottoman houses, while Laleli and Aksaray lack style but usually have lower prices. While Istanbul once had some of the cheapest accommodation in Europe, it's now among the most expensive.

Many mid-range hotels are very pleasant, the rooms equipped with TV, mini-bars, etc. One-star hotels are basic but comfortable. There are also *pansiyons*, often family-run and comfortable.

The Aegean resorts have large numbers of hotels, self-catering villas and apartments, many of which are used by tour operators. There are also the historic 'special' hotels, usually in old houses or *caravanserais*; they usually offer 3 to 5-star amenities, but often can't have lifts because of the age of the building.

It's important to book ahead in Istanbul, especially in July and August, when many Turkish tourists visit the city, and over the religious holidays of Şeker Bayram and Kurban Bayram. Low season is October–March (except Christmas and New Year), when most places lower their rates. It's worth checking online on discount hotel booking sites.

I'd like a single/double room. **Tek/çift yataklı bir oda istiyorum.**
What's the rate per night? **Bir gecelik oda ücreti ne kadar?**

AIRPORTS

The main airport is **Atatürk International Airport** (*Atatürk Havalimanı*, www.ataturkairport.com) near Yesilköy, 24km (15 miles) southwest of the city centre. A free shuttle bus links the international *(dışhatları)* and domestic *(içhatları)* terminals.

The municipality-owned coach service, Havataş (http://havatas.com) runs between the airport and the city centre, half-hourly between 4am and 1am, journey time around 40 minutes, but much longer during rush hour, and costs 11 TL. Buses depart from outside both international and domestic terminals to Taksim Square, in front of the Point Hotel. Taxis are a little faster and more convenient, 20–30 minutes to the city centre; around 40 TL. The cheapest, but slower option is the Metro to Askaray, then connect to the Tramway (short walk) which is handy for the old city.

Low-cost airlines – including Pegasus and regional airlines (Bora and Anadolu Jet) – use **Sabiha Gökçen International Airport**, Pendik, Asian Side (www.sgairport.com), 40km (25 miles) from Kadiköy and 50km (31 miles) from Taksim. It also has the Havataş bus to the city centre (approximately 75 minutes; 14 TL).

Airports for the Aegean are at **Izmir** (Adnan Menderes Airport; www.adnanmenderesairport.com) and **Bodrum** (Milas-Bodrum Airport; www.bodrum-airport.com) with charter international flights and domestic flights. Some Aegean resorts are reached from **Dalaman** (www.dalaman airport.aero/en). Transfers to hotels and resorts are available from these airports, but taxis are often extortionate – it is far better to use taxi apps where available.

APPS

Biletix: The official ticketing agents for events.
BiTaksi: Highly regarded taxi app.
IBB CepTrafik: Detailed journey planning app.
Istanbul Travel Guide: Useful app containing attraction information, maps, and augmented reality feature.
Uber: Globally popular taxi app.

BUDGETING FOR YOUR TRIP

Accommodation and meals are on a par with Western Europe. Expect to pay from £70 for a double in a *pansiyon*, above £100 for a mid-range or boutique hotel, considerably more in a 5-star deluxe.

Expect to pay at least £15–20 for a three-course meal in a mid-range restaurant, considerably more with alcohol. A bottle of wine in a restaurant starts at around 50 TL; in a bar a glass of wine at least 8 TL, with a small Efes beer from 5 TL.

The cost of public transport is minimal for buses, tram and ferries (around 4 TL basic rate and 2.15 TL with the Istanbulkart), and taxis are also inexpensive, at about 21–28 TL from Sultanhamet to Taksim although do ensure they use the meter and take the shortest route.

Most sites cost around 10 TL for entry, with the most expensive Hagia Sophia and Tokapı Palace at 30 TL each. Mosques do not charge admission but tips are appreciated. Consider buying a Istanbul Museum Pass (https://muze.gen.tr/MuseumPasses; 1/5/15-day available) to cut costs.

CAR HIRE (see also Driving)

A car is a liability in traffic-packed Istanbul, but if you plan to travel further afield, renting a car is sensible, as the rail system is not extensive. Car-hire rates vary – local companies charge less than international chains, and it's possible to pay as little as £25 per day. You can get good rates by booking and paying before you leave home, through the UK office of an international company. Check that the rate includes Collision Damage Waiver, unlimited mileage and VAT (KDV in Turkey). Hire-car insurance never covers you for broken windscreens and burst tyres. Unless you hire a four-wheel-drive, you will not be insured for driving on unsurfaced roads. You must be over 21 and you will need your passport, a valid driver's licence (with photo) held for at least 12 months, and a major credit card.

CLIMATE

Istanbul has a typical Mediterranean, temperate climate with warm, dry summers and cool, wet winters. July and August are the hottest months.

The best time to visit is April–June when the days are warm, and the shores of the Bosphorus are bright with spring flowers. Winter is generally cold, wet and uncomfortable. Snow is not uncommon in the north but rarely settles for more than a few days. The southern Aegean can have clear, sunny days, even in January.

Average daily maximum and minimum temperatures for Istanbul:

	J	F	M	A	M	J	J	A	S	O	N	D
°C max	8	10	12	17	22	26	28	28	25	20	15	11
°C min	3	4	5	8	12	16	18	18	15	12	8	5
°F max	46	50	53	62	71	79	82	82	77	68	59	51
°F min	37	39	41	46	53	60	65	65	59	53	46	41

CRIME AND SAFETY (See also Emergencies and Police)

You are far less likely to be a victim of crime in Turkey than you are in Western Europe or North America. Nevertheless, take the usual precautions against theft, keeping valuables tucked away out of sight, and be aware of pickpockets in crowded areas and on public transport. In poorer areas, such as Balat, avoid walking down unlit streets alone at night, and be careful when returning from late-night bars around Beyoğlu. Report any theft or loss to the police. If your passport is lost or stolen, inform your consulate. It's obligatory to carry your passport at all times, so keep a photocopy of relevant pages at your hotel in case of theft. Drug use or trafficking is punished severely; avoid it at all costs. Bomb attacks in Istanbul and resorts on the Aegean coast are of concern, but the chances of being involved are tiny.

DRIVING (See also Car Hire and Emergencies)

The standard of driving can be erratic so it's not advisable to drive in Istanbul. If you bring your own vehicle, you need a full driver's licence, an International Motor Insurance Certificate and 'Green Card' (make sure it's valid for the Asian sector if you plan to cross the Dardanelles or Bosphorus), and a Vehicle Registration Document. An official nationality plate must be displayed near the rear number plate, and headlamp beams must be adjusted for driving on the right. Check the website of Turkish Touring and Automobile Club (www.turing.org.tr) for information on driving licences and permits.

Seat belts must be worn in both front and back seats; on-the-spot fines can be issued for non-compliance. A red warning triangle and fire extinguisher must be carried. Motorcycle riders and passengers must wear crash helmets. The minimum legal age for driving is 18, and laws prohibiting drinking and driving are strictly enforced.

(international) driving permit **(uluslararası) ehliyet**
car registration papers **araba ruhsatı**
Green Card **yeşil kartı**
Can I park here? **Buraya park edebilir miyim?**
Are we on the right road for…? **…için doğru yolda mıyız?**
Full tank, please. **Dodurun, lütfen.**
I've broken down. **Arabam arzalandı.**

Rules of the road. Drive on the right, and overtake on the left. Speed limits are 120km/h (75mph) on motorways, 90km/h (55mph) on highways and 40 or 50km/h (25 or 30mph) in towns. Traffic joining from the right has priority, unless signs or markings indicate otherwise. There are fast, empty toll motorways between Istanbul, Edirne and Ankara and around İzmir

Fuel. In western Turkey there are plenty of petrol (gas) stations, and many are open 24 hours, but there are very few service stations on the toll motorways. Petrol is very expensive.

Parking. Look for signs saying *park yapilmaz* or *park yasaktır* (no parking) – police enforce regulations rigidly; they tow away illegally parked vehicles within a very short time and drivers have to pay a fine to retrieve them. Look for an official car park *(otopark)*.

Traffic police. You can recognise the Turkish *Trafik Polisi* by their black-and-white baseball-style caps and two-tone Renault patrol cars. They patrol city streets and highways, and have the power to issue on-the-spot fines for traffic offences. Call 154 for help.

Breakdown. Most towns have a mechanic. Larger towns and cities have full repair shops and towing services. For rental cars there will be a 24-hour emergency telephone number, and the company will arrange repairs or a replacement. For tyre repairs, look for a sign saying *lastikçi*, usually painted on an old tyre at the roadside.

Road signs. Main roads are well signposted; sights of interest to tourists are marked by special yellow signs with black lettering. Below are some common Turkish signs:

Çikis exit
Dıkkat caution
Dinlenme Alani rest area
Dur stop
Gırılmez no entry
Park yapilmaz no parking
Sehir merkezı city centre
Tekyön one way
Yavas slow
Yolver give way
Yol yapimi roadworks
24 Saat Açik open 24 hrs

ELECTRICITY

220-volt, 50-cycle current. An adaptor is needed for Continental-style two-pin sockets; American 110-volt appliances require a transformer.

EMBASSIES AND CONSULATES

Embassies are in the capital city of Ankara, but most countries maintain consulates in Istanbul:

Canada: 15/F Tekfen Tower, 209 Buyukdere Caddesi, Levent 4; tel: 0212-385 9700, www.international.gc.ca/country-pays/turkiye/istanbul.aspx.

UK: Meşrutiyet Caddesi 42, Tepebaşı, Beyoğlu; tel: 0212-334-6400, www.

gov.uk/world/organisations/british-consulate-general-istanbul.

US: Poligon Mahallesi 75, Sariyer Caddesi; tel: 0212-335 9000, https://tr.usembassy.gov/embassy-consulates/istanbul.

EMERGENCIES

Tourist police **0212 527 4503**

Police **155**

Ambulance **112**

Fire **110**

GETTING THERE

Scheduled flights from the UK. The national airline, Turkish Airlines (UK reservations www.turkishairlines.com), flies to Istanbul four times daily from London Heathrow, four times weekly or even daily in high season from Manchester and twice weekly from Birmingham. There are daily direct flights by British Airways (www.ba.com). EasyJet flies to Bodrum and Izmir from Gatwick (www.easyjet.com) as does Pegasus Airlines (www.flypgs.com), which also has domestic flights around the country.

Scheduled flights from the US and Canada. Turkish Airlines has regular non-stop flights from New York, Los Angeles and Chicago to Istanbul. (www.turkishairlines.com)

Charter flights and package tours from the UK and Ireland. Available from a number of British cities to Izmir, Bodrum and Dalaman (on the south coast near Marmaris) in summer, available as flight only or as part of a hotel or self-catering package holiday.

By road. From the UK the main overland route passes through Germany, Austria, Hungary, Romania and Bulgaria. The distance from London to Istanbul is approximately 3,000km (1,870 miles), which takes at least four days of steady driving.

By rail. Allow approximately three days from London to Istanbul. The InterRail Global pass allows various periods of unlimited travel in 30 European countries, including Turkey (for details see www.raileurope.co.uk). The best single website for planning is www.seat61.com.

GUIDES AND TOURS

Official English-speaking guides can be hired through the local tourist office and through travel agencies and the better hotels. They are usually friendly and knowledgeable, and can prove invaluable if your time is limited. Freelance guides also hang around at the entrance to Topkapı Palace (make sure you agree on a price and ensure they are official, and that their English is good enough). There are increasing numbers of special interest tours: eg archaeology, Byzantine art and tours of historic Jewish sites. Les Arts Turcs (Incili çavus Sokak 19, Sultanahmet; www.lesartsturcs.com) is a fantastic little place with friendly staff, organising specialist tours and events.

You can also combine a city break in Istanbul with a resort holiday in the Aegean, or 14 days of cruising on a *gullet* (sailing boat).

HEALTH AND MEDICAL CARE

There is no free health care for visitors to Turkey so take out adequate insurance. However, Turkish hospitals are not prohibitively expensive, and they offer excellent treatment. Note that an EHIC card is only valid for EU countries, so can't be used in Turkey.

The main health hazards are the sun and the risk of diarrhoea, so use sunblock and a shady hat and be careful with food and drinks. Stick to bottled drinking water; ice will be fine in a reputable venue otherwise avoid it. Top restaurants may serve filtered water at the table, which is fine. Take a pack of wet wipes for washing hands. For minor ailments, seek advice from a pharmacy *(eczane)*, usually open during shopping hours. After hours, at least one is open all night, called the *nöbet* or *nöbetci*, its location is posted in the window of all other pharmacies.

Vaccinations. There are no compulsory requirements, but vaccinations for tetanus, polio, typhoid and hepatitis A are recommended.

Where's the nearest pharmacy? **En yakın eczane nerededir?**
Where can I find a doctor/ a dentist? **Nereden bir doktor/bir dişci bulabilirim?**

an ambulance/hospital **bir ambülans/hastane**
sunburn **güneş yanığı**
a fever/an upset stomach **ateş/mide bozulması**

LANGUAGE

Very few Istanbullus speak English, except for those working in tourist-related areas, and along the Aegean coast. Local people will naturally welcome any attempt you make to speak their language. Below is the pronunciation of some Turkish letters:

c like **j** in jam
ç like **ch** in **ch**ip
ğ almost silent; lengthens the preceding vowel
h always clearly pronounced
ı like **i** in **si**r
j like **s** in pleasure
ö approx. like **ur** in f**u**r (like German *ö*)
ş like **sh** in **sh**ell
ü approx. like **ew** in f**ew** (like German *ü*)

We'd like an English-speaking guide **İngilizce bilen bir rehber istiyoruz.**
I need an English interpreter. **İngilizce bilen bir çevirmene ihtiyacım var.**

LGBTQ+ TRAVELLERS

Although homosexuality is officially illegal in Turkey, there are plenty of gay bars and clubs in Istanbul, with homophobic trouble practically unheard of. Look out for magazines such as *Time Out Istanbul*, which offer good, up-to-date listings. Bear in mind that 'rent boys' are relatively common and may target unknowing foreigners. Transsexuality is also fairly common in gay clubs. Avoid going with a new 'friend' to a bar or club of their choice –

prices could be significantly inflated and you are forced to pay. The annual Gay Pride march takes place in June, although it has been officially banned since 2015.

MONEY

Currency. The Turk Lira (TL). Coins (*kuruş*) are in 1, 5, 10, 25 and 1 TL denominations. Notes are in 1, 5, 10, 20, 50, 100 and 200 TL units.

Banks and currency exchange *(banka; kambiyo; döviz)*. Banks generally open 8.30am–noon, 1.30–5pm Mon–Fri (many stay open at lunch time). Rates of exchange and commission vary slightly, but in general bureaux de change have better rates than banks. The rate in Turkey is always better than in the UK. You can also change cash and traveller's cheques at the PTT office.

ATMs. A credit/debit card and an ATM is the fastest and easiest way to get cash.

Credit cards *(kredi kartı)*. Major credit and debit cards are increasingly accepted in hotels, restaurants, tourist shops and car-hire companies. Some shops may ask you to pay a premium. Most outlets require you to input your PIN at point of sale.

I want to change some pounds/dollars. **Sterlin/dolar bozdurmak istiyorum.**

Do you accept traveller's cheques? **Seyahat çeki kabul eder misiniz?**

Can I pay with this credit card? **Bu kredi kartımla ödeyebilir miyim?**

OPENING TIMES

Banks: Mon–Fri 8.30am–noon, 1.30–5pm (some daily).

Currency exchange offices (döviz): daily 8am–8pm.

Museums and major attractions: generally Tue–Sun 9.30am–5pm (some may close later in summer).

Post offices (PTT): main offices Mon–Sat 9am–5pm.

Shops: Mon–Sat 9.30am–7pm. Many stay open later and on Sunday, especially around Istiklal Caddesi. Grand Bazaar: Mon–Sat 8am–7pm.

POLICE (see also Emergencies)

The Turkish police's reputation for corruption is gradually improving. Officers wear dark-blue trousers with pale-blue shirts. Motorbike police wear black with red edging. Tourist Police (Yerebatan Caddesi, Sultanahmet, tel: 0212-528 5369) have a 'Tourism Police' logo on their backs. To call the police in an emergency dial **155**.

A stamp for this letter/postcard, please. **Bu mektup/kart için bir pul, lütfen.**
express (special delivery) **ekspres**
airmail/ **uçak ile**
registered **taahütlü**

PUBLIC HOLIDAYS

Secular holidays occur on the same date each year, religious holidays are calculated by the Islamic authorities according to the lunar calendar, and thus occur about 11 days earlier each year. Banks, post offices, government offices and many other businesses will be closed on the following secular holidays:

1 January *Yılbaşı*: New Year's Day
23 April *Ulusal Egemenlik ve Çocuk Bayramı*: National Sovereignty and Children's Day.
19 May *Gençlik ve Spor Günü*: Youth and Sports Day (Atatürk's Birthday)
30 August *Zafer Bayramı*: Victory Day.)
29 October *Cumhuriyet Bayramı*: Republic Day.
10 November Anniversary of Atatürk's death

There are two national religious holidays (*Şeker Bayramı* and *Kurban Bayramı*), marked by three and four days off respectively. Most museums and attractions will be closed for the first two days, and shops for one or two, depending on its location. Inter-city transport (planes, coaches and buses) will be booked solid then and hotels will be busy.

RELIGION

The national religion is Islam. It's important to be mindful of dress codes in mosques – no shorts or bare shoulders, and women need to cover their hair. Istanbul also has Christian and Jewish minorities, and there are a number of churches and synagogues.

TELEPHONES

Turkey is on the GSM mobile network (US visitors need a tri-band phone). You can make domestic and international calls from public phones in PTT offices, or phone boxes on the street. They accept credit cards or telephone cards (*telekart*), which can be bought at the ptt and some newsstands and kiosks. For cheaper international calls, buy a calling card from newsstands, which can also be used from your hotel room. There are also kiosks in post offices and private phone offices (*telefon ofisi*), the latter are more expensive.

For intercity calls (including to Üsküdar across the Bosphorus), dial 0, then the area code (212 in European Istanbul; 216 on the Asian side), then the number. For international calls, dial 00, then the country code and the full number including area code. Turkey's country code is 90. Making and receiving mobile phone calls is expensive, but you can buy a SIM card (try Turkcell or Vodafone), valid for up to 7 days – providing it is the first time you've brought your phone into the country. If your stay is for longer, you will have to register your phone, which may take some time to be validated.

TIME ZONES

GMT plus 2 hours in winter, GMT plus 3 hours in summer, making it 2 hours ahead of the UK all year. Clocks go forward on the last Sunday in March, and back on the last Sunday in October.

TIPPING

In a restaurant tip 10–15 percent, even if the bill says service is included *(servis dahildir)*. Often waiters rely solely on their tips as income. Hotel porters should get around 1–2 TL; 10–15 percent is the norm in barber shops and Turkish baths, and a few coins, worth around 10p, should be left in public toilets, although many have a set fee of decidedly more. Taxi drivers don't expect a tip, but it is usual to round up the fare. *Dolmuş* drivers never expect a tip.

TOILETS

Public toilets are usually found in museums and tourist attractions and near mosques. They are occasionally of the hole-in-the-floor variety, and may lack toilet paper, so carry a packet of tissues. Paper should be put in the bin provided, not in the toilet. *Kadınlar* or *Bayanlar* (Ladies) and *Erkekler* or *Baylar* (Gentlemen).

Where are the toilets? **Tuvaletler nerede?**

TOURIST INFORMATION

The main Ministry of Tourism offices in Istanbul are:
Sultanahmet Meydani (by the tram stop), tel: 0212-518 1802/8754; Sirkeci station, tel: 0212-511 5888; opposite Hilton Hotel, Elmadag, tel: 0212-233 0592; Merkez Caddesi 6, opposite Atatürk Kültür Merkezi, Taksim Square, tel: 0212-2465 313; Atatürk Airport arrivals.
Turkish Tourist Offices abroad:
UK: 3rd Floor, Craven House 121 Kingsway, London WC2B 6PA, tel: 020-7839 7802
US: 825 3rd Avenue Floor 5, New York, NY 10022, tel: 212-687-2194, 5055 Wilshire Blvd. Suite 850, Los Angeles, CA, 90036, tel: 323-937 8066.

TRANSPORT

Istanbul's public transport system is run by IETT (www.iett.gov.tr), which integrates buses, metro, tramway and light rail. Most services run from 6am to after midnight.

Fares. The single fare for bus, metro, tram, funicular, Tünel, ferry is 4 TL, but it is cheaper to buy an **Istanbulkart** or **Abkil** transit pass (a stainless steel button with an electronic chip). Single fare tokens *(jeton)*, Akbil transit Pass and Istanbulkart are sold at the vending machines at the major bus stops, metro and tram stations, ferry docks or at the newspapers stands in Eminönü, Taksim Square, Beyazit and other transport hubs.

Buses. City buses are cheap and frequent, but can be crowded. They are useful for a some major sights and longer trips in and out of the city. There are also private lines on the more popular routes where you can pay in cash.

Trams. The sleek service tram, the T1 Bağcılar-Kabataş, runs every 10 minutes along European shore. Useful stops include Sultanahmet (for Blue Mosque, Hagia Sophia and Topkapı Palace), Beyazit (Grand Bazaar) and Fındıklı (Istanbul Modern). At the Kabataş Pier there is a funicular that runs uphill to Taksim Square and catamaran ferry dock. A restored 19th-century tram runs along Istiklal Caddesi from Tünel to Taksim Square. Another runs from Usküdar down to Kadiköy on the Asian side.

Metro. There are several metro lines but the most useful to visitors is M1 from Aksaray Square through the mammoth Otogar (inter-city bus station) to Atatürk Airport.

Funiculars. Istanbul's tiny underground train, the Tünel, climbs the steep hill from Karaköy on the north side of the Galata Bridge to Pera. Trains leave every few minutes and take only 90 seconds to reach the top. A second funicular links Kabataş ferry port on the Bosphorus with Taksim Square.

Trains. The suburban rail service is currently suspended due to the opening of a new Marmaray system scheduled for 2015. The only line in operation before then connects stations at Yenikapı and Sirkeci in Old Istanbul in Europe with the Üskudar and Ayrılık Çeşmesi in Asia via a rail tunnel beneath the Bosphorus.

Ferries. The traditional big ferryboats operated by Istanbul Şehir Hatları depart from Eminönü for the Bosphorus and Golden Horn cruises, and to Üsküdar and Kadıköy (the Asian side), and Princes' Islands. There is also a private co-operative, TurYol (www.turyol.com), from the west of Galata Bridge, which offers a number of different Bosphorus trips. There are also ferries from Beşiktas and Kabataş.

Sea bus catamaran. Sleek catamarans *(deniz otobüsü)* zoom across the waterways, and out to Princes' Islands several times daily. There are also Sea of Marmara routes to Yalova and Bandirma on the southern shore.

Dolmuş. A large yellow minibus that shuttles along a set route for a fixed fare. The destination is shown on the windscreen. The driver leaves the starting point when all seats are taken, then drops passengers off along the way (*dolmuş* stops are marked by a sign with a 'D'). Call out '*inecek var!*' when you want to get off.

Taxis. Taxis are yellow, and mostly powered by clean-burning natural gas. They can be hailed in the street, picked up at a rank or ordered by phone. It's better to hail one that is already on the move, rather than those loitering outside tourist sites. Taxis have meters and are required by law to use them. Most drivers are honest, but a few may try to rip you off by 'adjusting' the meter or doing tricks with your money. Night and day rates are the same. If you take a taxi across the Bosphorus Bridge, you also have to pay the bridge toll. Few drivers speak English, so it's worth writing your destination on a piece of paper.

VISAS AND ENTRY REQUIREMENTS

Visas. All travellers need a passport valid for at least six months. Travellers from many countries, including the UK, do not need a visa for stays of up to 90 days. Visas for stays longer than 90 days need to be applied for via the Electronic Visa Application System (www.evisa.gov.tr) and pay with a credit or debit card.

WEBSITES AND INTERNET ACCESS

www.gototurkey.co.uk: The UK's official Turkish tourism site.

www.iksv.org: Organisers of most arts and culture festivals.

www.turkeytravelplanner.com: American-targeted site with practical tips and links to vetted service providers.

www.muze.gov.tr: Information about all the museums and sites in Turkey.

In addition to sleek cafés with fast wifi, tiny internet cafés are scattered around the city centre, especially in the Beyoğlu area. Charges are around 2 TL per hour.

Index

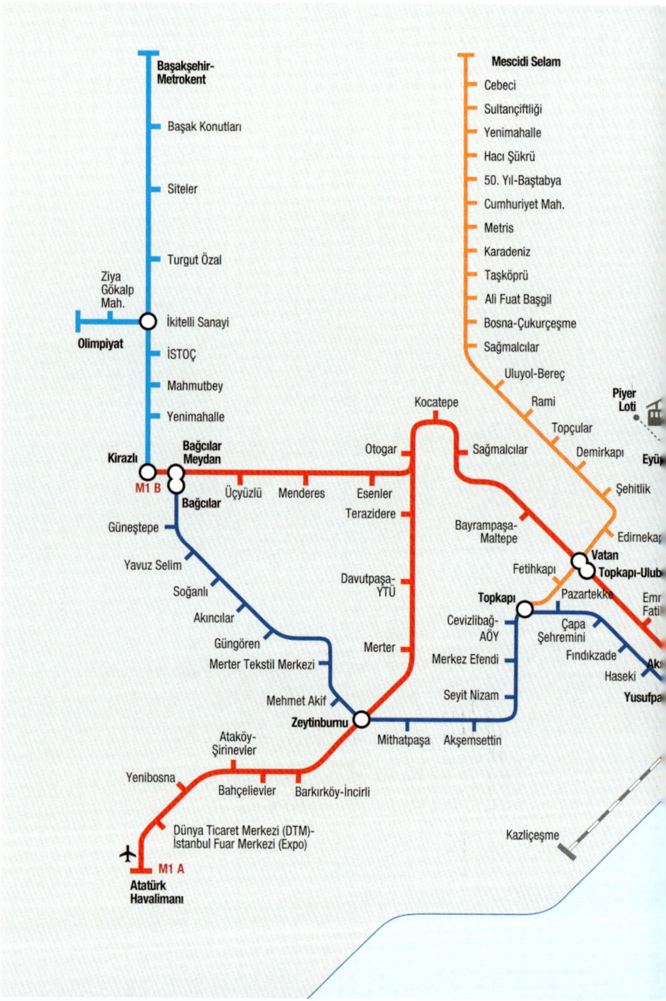

Başakşehir-Metrokent
Başak Konutları
Siteler
Turgut Özal
Ziya Gökalp Mah.
Olimpiyat
İkitelli Sanayi
İSTOÇ
Mahmutbey
Yenimahalle
Kirazlı
M1 B
Bağcılar Meydan
Bağcılar
Üçyüzlü
Menderes
Esenler
Otogar
Kocatepe
Sağmalcılar
Terazidere
Güneştepe
Yavuz Selim
Soğanlı
Akıncılar
Güngören
Merter Tekstil Merkezi
Davutpaşa-YTÜ
Merter
Mehmet Akif
Zeytinburnu
Mithatpaşa
Akşemsettin
Seyit Nizam
Merkez Efendi
Cevizlibağ-AÖY
Topkapı
Pazartekke
Çapa Şehremini
Fındıkzade
Haseki
Fetihkapı
Vatan
Bayrampaşa-Maltepe
Mescidi Selam
Cebeci
Sultançiftliği
Yenimahalle
Hacı Şükrü
50. Yıl-Baştabya
Cumhuriyet Mah.
Metris
Karadeniz
Taşköprü
Ali Fuat Başgil
Bosna-Çukurçeşme
Sağmalcılar
Uluyol-Bereç
Rami
Topçular
Demirkapı
Şehitlik
Piyer Loti
Ataköy-Şirinevler
Yenibosna
Bahçelievler
Barkırköy-İncirli
Dünya Ticaret Merkezi (DTM)-İstanbul Fuar Merkezi (Expo)
M1 A
Atatürk Havalimanı
Kazlıçeşme

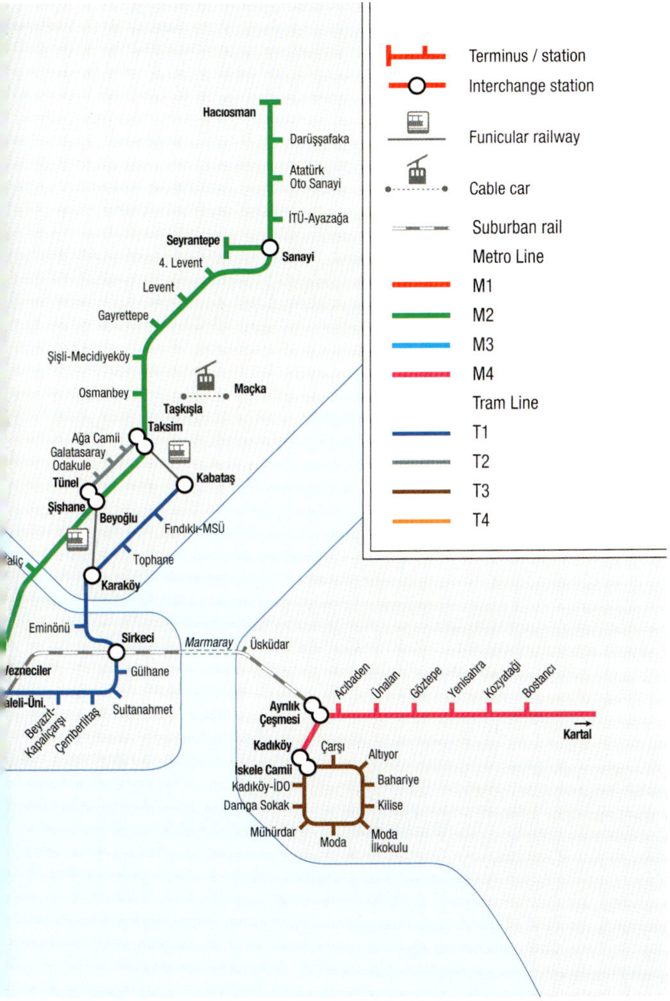
Terminus / station
Interchange station
Funicular railway
Cable car
Suburban rail
Metro Line
M1
M2
M3
M4
Tram Line
T1
T2
T3
T4
Hacıosman
Darüşşafaka
Atatürk Oto Sanayi
İTÜ-Ayazağa
Seyrantepe
Sanayi
4. Levent
Levent
Gayrettepe
Şişli-Mecidiyeköy
Osmanbey
Maçka
Taşkışla
Taksim
Ağa Camii
Galatasaray
Odakule
Tünel
Şişhane
Beyoğlu
Kabataş
Fındıklı-MSÜ
Tophane
Karaköy
Eminönü
Sirkeci
Marmaray
Üsküdar
Gülhane
Sultanahmet
Beyazıt-Kapalıçarşı
Çemberlitaş
Acıbaden
Ünalan
Göztepe
Yenisahra
Kozyatağı
Bostancı
Ayrılık Çeşmesi
Kartal
Kadıköy
Çarşı
Altıyor
İskele Camii
Kadıköy-İDO
Bahariye
Damga Sokak
Kilise
Mühürdar
Moda
Moda İlkokulu

THE **MINI** ROUGH GUIDE TO **ISTANBUL**
& THE AEGEAN COAST

First Edition 2025

Editor: Siobhan Warwicker
Author: Daniel Stables
Picture Editor: Piotr Kala
Picture Manager: Tom Smyth
Cartography Update: Katie Bennett
Layout: Grzegorz Madejak
Production Operations Manager: Katie Bennett
Publishing Technology Manager: Rebeka Davies
Head of Publishing: Sarah Clark
Photography Credits: All images Shutterstock except: Dreamstime 12BL, 51, 108; Frank Noon/Apa Publications 12CR, 86, 88, 93, 110, 111, 112, 114; Ggia 12TL, 55; iStock 12TL, 12TR, 13T, 20, 23, 30, 41, 54, 70, 76, 82, 84, 94, 97; Public domain 25, 26; Rebecca Erol/Apa Publications 6, 10, 12BR, 13CT, 13CB, 24, 34, 36, 38, 43, 44, 46, 48, 52, 58, 61, 62, 65, 68, 72, 74, 79, 80, 98, 100, 103, 105, 107, 115, 116; Turkish Tourism 28
Cover Credits: The Blue Mosque **iStock**

About the author

Daniel Stables is a travel writer based in Manchester, UK. He writes travel articles for National Geographic and the BBC, and his debut narrative travel book, *Fiesta: A Journey Through Festivity* is coming out in early 2026. He also hosts a podcast, *Hungry Ghosts*, about food and travel. You can find his work on X @DanStables, Instagram @DanStabs, or at his website, danielstables.co.uk.

Distribution

UK, Ireland and Europe: Apa Publications (UK) Ltd; sales@roughguides.com
United States and Canada: Ingram Publisher Services; ips@ingramcontent.com
Australia and New Zealand: Booktopia; retailer@booktopia.com.au
Worldwide: Apa Publications (UK) Ltd; sales@roughguides.com

Special Sales, Content Licensing and CoPublishing

Rough Guides can be purchased in bulk quantities at discounted prices. We can create special editions, personalised jackets and corporate imprints tailored to your needs. sales@roughguides.com; http://roughguides.com

Printed in Czech Republic

This book was produced using **Typefi** automated publishing software.

Contact us

Every effort has been made to provide accurate information in this publication, but changes are inevitable. The publisher cannot be held responsible for any resulting loss, inconvenience or injury sustained by any traveller as a result of information or advice contained in the guide. We would appreciate it if readers would call our attention to any errors or outdated information, or if you feel we've left something out. Please send your comments with the subject line "Rough Guide Mini Istanbul & the Aegean Coast Update" to mail@uk.roughguides.com.